Computer Forensics

Contents

Chapter 1

Computer forensics

Computer forensics analysis is not limited only to computer media

Computer forensics (sometimes known as **computer forensic science**[1]) is a branch of digital forensic science pertaining to evidence found in computers and digital storage media. The goal of computer forensics is to examine digital media in a forensically sound manner with the aim of identifying, preserving, recovering, analyzing and presenting facts and opinions about the digital information.

Although it is most often associated with the investigation of a wide variety of computer crime, computer forensics may also be used in civil proceedings. The discipline involves similar techniques and principles to data recovery, but with additional guidelines and practices designed to create a legal audit trail.

Evidence from computer forensics investigations is usually subjected to the same guidelines and practices of other digital evidence. It has been used in a number of high-profile cases and is becoming widely accepted as reliable within U.S. and European court systems.

1.1 Overview

In the early 1980s personal computers became more accessible to consumers, leading to their increased use in criminal activity (for example, to help commit fraud). At the same time, several new "computer crimes" were recognized (such as hacking). The discipline of computer forensics emerged during this time as a method to recover and investigate digital evidence for use in court. Since then computer crime and computer related crime has grown, and has jumped 67% between 2002 and 2003.[2] Today it is used to investigate a wide variety of crime, including child pornography, fraud, espionage, cyberstalking, murder and rape. The discipline also features in civil proceedings as a form of information gathering (for example, Electronic discovery)

Forensic techniques and expert knowledge are used to explain the current state of a *digital artifact*; such as a computer system, storage medium (e.g. hard disk or CD-ROM), an electronic document (e.g. an email message or JPEG image).[3] The scope of a forensic analysis can vary from simple information retrieval to reconstructing a series of events. In a 2002 book *Computer Forensics* authors Kruse and Heiser define computer forensics as involving "the preservation, identification, extraction, documentation and interpretation of computer data".[4] They go on to describe the discipline as "more of an art than a science", indicating that forensic methodology is backed by flexibility and extensive domain knowledge. However, while several methods can be used to extract evidence from a given computer the strategies used by law enforcement are fairly rigid and lacking the flexibility found in the civilian world.[5]

1.2 Use as evidence

In court, computer forensic evidence is subject to the usual requirements for digital evidence. This requires that information be authentic, reliably obtained, and admissible.[6] Different countries have specific guidelines and practices for evidence recovery. In the United Kingdom, examiners often follow Association of Chief Police Officers guidelines that help ensure the authenticity and integrity of evidence. While voluntary, the guidelines are widely accepted in British courts.

Computer forensics has been used as evidence in criminal law since the mid-1980s, some notable examples include:[7]

- BTK Killer: Dennis Rader was convicted of a string of serial killings that occurred over a period of sixteen years. Towards the end of this period, Rader sent letters to the police on a floppy disk. Metadata within the documents implicated an author named "Dennis" at "Christ Lutheran Church"; this evidence helped lead to Rader's arrest.

- Joseph E. Duncan III: A spreadsheet recovered from Duncan's computer contained evidence that showed him planning his crimes. Prosecutors used this to show premeditation and secure the death penalty.[8]

- Sharon Lopatka: Hundreds of emails on Lopatka's computer lead investigators to her killer, Robert Glass.[7]

- Corcoran Group: This case confirmed parties' duties to preserve digital evidence when litigation has commenced or is reasonably anticipated. Hard drives were analyzed by a computer forensics expert who could not find relevant emails the Defendants should have had. Though the expert found no evidence of deletion on the hard drives, evidence came out that the defendants were found to have intentionally destroyed emails, and misled and failed to disclose material facts to the plaintiffs and the court.

- Dr. Conrad Murray: Dr. Conrad Murray, the doctor of the deceased Michael Jackson, was convicted partially by digital evidence on his computer. This evidence included medical documentation showing lethal amounts of propofol.

1.3 Forensic process

Main article: Digital forensic process

Computer forensic investigations usually follow the standard digital forensic process or phases: acquisition, examination, analysis and reporting. Investigations are performed on static data (i.e. acquired images) rather than "live" systems. This is a change from early forensic practices where a lack of specialist tools led to investigators commonly working on live data.

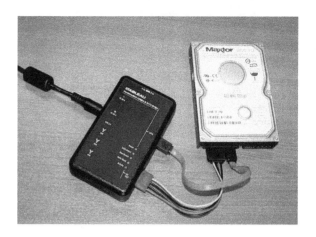

A portable Tableau write blocker attached to a Hard Drive

1.3.1   Techniques

A number of techniques are used during computer forensics investigations and much has been written on the many techniques used by law enforcement in particular.See, e.g., "Defending Child Pornography Cases".

Cross-drive analysis A forensic technique that correlates information found on multiple hard drives. The process, still being researched, can be used to identify social networks and to perform anomaly detection.[9][10]

Live analysis The examination of computers from within the operating system using custom forensics or existing sysadmin tools to extract evidence. The practice is useful when dealing with Encrypting File Systems, for example, where the encryption keys may be collected and, in some instances, the logical hard drive volume may be imaged (known as a live acquisition) before the computer is shut down.

Deleted files A common technique used in computer forensics is the recovery of deleted files. Modern forensic software have their own tools for recovering or carving out deleted data.[11] Most operating systems and file systems do not always erase physical file data, allowing investigators to reconstruct it from the physical disk sectors. File carving involves searching for known file headers within the disk image and reconstructing deleted materials.

Stochastic forensics A method which uses stochastic properties of the computer system to investigate activities lacking digital artifacts. Its chief use is to investigate data theft.

Steganography

One of the techniques used to hide data is via steganography, the process of hiding data inside of a picture or digital image. An example would be to hide pornographic images of children or other information that a given criminal does not want to have discovered. Computer forensics professionals can fight this by looking at the hash of the file and comparing it to the original image (if available.) While the image appears exactly the same, the hash changes as the data changes. In Forensic examination, Steganalysis is used to get the details of Steganographic contents.[12]

1.3.2 Volatile data

When seizing evidence, if the machine is still active, any information stored solely in RAM that is not recovered before powering down may be lost.[8] One application of "live analysis" is to recover RAM data (for example, using Microsoft's COFEE tool, windd, WindowsSCOPE) prior to removing an exhibit. CaptureGUARD Gateway bypasses Windows login for locked computers, allowing for the analysis and acquisition of physical memory on a locked computer.

RAM can be analyzed for prior content after power loss, because the electrical charge stored in the memory cells takes time to dissipate, an effect exploited by the cold boot attack. The length of time that data is recoverable is increased by low temperatures and higher cell voltages. Holding unpowered RAM below −60 °C helps preserve residual data by an order of magnitude, improving the chances of successful recovery. However, it can be impractical to do this during a field examination.[13]

Some of the tools needed to extract volatile data, however, require that a computer be in a forensic lab, both to maintain a legitimate chain of evidence, and to facilitate work on the machine. If necessary, law enforcement applies techniques to move a live, running desktop computer. These include a mouse jiggler, which moves the mouse rapidly in small movements and prevents the computer from going to sleep accidentally. Usually, an uninterruptible power supply (UPS) provides power during transit.

However, one of the easiest ways to capture data is by actually saving the RAM data to disk. Various file systems that have journaling features such as NTFS and ReiserFS keep a large portion of the RAM data on the main storage media during operation, and these page files can be reassembled to reconstruct what was in RAM at that time.[14]

1.3.3 Analysis tools

See also: List of digital forensics tools

A number of open source and commercial tools exist for computer forensics investigation. Typical forensic analysis includes a manual review of material on the media, reviewing the Windows registry for suspect information, discovering and cracking passwords, keyword searches for topics related to the crime, and extracting e-mail and pictures for review.[7]

1.4 Certifications

There are several computer forensics certifications available, such as the ISFCE Certified Computer Examiner, Digital Forensics Investigation Professional (DFIP) and IACRB Certified Computer Forensics Examiner.

IACIS (the International Association of Computer Investigative Specialists) offers the Certified Computer Forensic Examiner (CFCE) program.

Asian School of Cyber Laws offers international level certifications in Digital Evidence Analysis and in Digital Forensic Investigation. These Courses are available in online and class room mode.

Many commercial based forensic software companies are now also offering proprietary certifications on their products. For example Guidance Software offering the (EnCE) certification on their tool EnCase, AccessData offering (ACE) certification on their tool FTK, PassMark Software offering (OCE) certification on their tool OSForensics, and X-Ways Software Technology offering (X-PERT) certification for their software, X-Ways Forensics.[15]

1.5 See also

- Counter forensics
- Certified Computer Examiner
- Certified Forensic Computer Examiner
- Cryptanalysis
- Data remanence
- Disk encryption
- Encryption
- Hidden file and hidden directory

- Information technology audit
- MAC times
- Steganalysis
- United States v. Arnold

1.6 References

[1] Michael G. Noblett; Mark M. Pollitt; Lawrence A. Presley (October 2000). "Recovering and examining computer forensic evidence". Retrieved 26 July 2010.

[2] Leigland, R (September 2004). "A Formalization of Digital Forensics" (PDF).

[3] A Yasinsac; RF Erbacher; DG Marks; MM Pollitt (2003). "Computer forensics education". IEEE Security & Privacy. CiteSeerX: 10.1.1.1.9510.

[4] Warren G. Kruse; Jay G. Heiser (2002). *Computer forensics: incident response essentials*. Addison-Wesley. p. 392. ISBN 0-201-70719-5. Retrieved 6 December 2010.

[5] Gunsch, G (August 2002). "An Examination of Digital Forensic Models" (PDF).

[6] Adams, R. (2012). "'The Advanced Data Acquisition Model (ADAM): A process model for digital forensic practice".

[7] Casey, Eoghan (2004). *Digital Evidence and Computer Crime, Second Edition*. Elsevier. ISBN 0-12-163104-4.

[8] Various (2009). Eoghan Casey, ed. *Handbook of Digital Forensics and Investigation*. Academic Press. p. 567. ISBN 0-12-374267-6. Retrieved 27 August 2010.

[9] Garfinkel, S. (August 2006). "Forensic Feature Extraction and Cross-Drive Analysis" (PDF).

[10] "EXP-SA: Prediction and Detection of Network Membership through Automated Hard Drive Analysis".

[11] Aaron Phillip; David Cowen; Chris Davis (2009). *Hacking Exposed: Computer Forensics*. McGraw Hill Professional. p. 544. ISBN 0-07-162677-8. Retrieved 27 August 2010.

[12] Dunbar, B (January 2001). "A detailed look at Steganographic Techniques and their use in an Open-Systems Environment".

[13] J. Alex Halderman, Seth D. Schoen, Nadia Heninger, William Clarkson, William Paul, Joseph A. Calandrino, Ariel J. Feldman, Jacob Appelbaum, and Edward W. Felten (2008-02-21). "Lest We Remember: Cold Boot Attacks on Encryption Keys". Princeton University. Retrieved 2009-11-20.

[14] Geiger, M (March 2005). "Evaluating Commercial Counter-Forensic Tools" (PDF).

[15] "X-PERT Certification Program". X-pert.eu. Retrieved 2015-11-26.

1.7 Further reading

- A Practice Guide to Computer Forensics, First Edition (Paperback) by David Benton (Author), Frank Grindstaff (Author)
- Casey, Eoghan; Stellatos, Gerasimos J. (2008). "The impact of full disk encryption on digital forensics". *Operating Systems Review* **42** (3): 93–98. doi:10.1145/1368506.1368519.
- YiZhen Huang and YangJing Long (2008). "Demosaicking recognition with applications in digital photo authentication based on a quadratic pixel correlation model" (PDF). *Proc. IEEE Conference on Computer Vision and Pattern Recognition*: 1–8.
- Incident Response and Computer Forensics, Second Edition (Paperback) by Chris Prosise (Author), Kevin Mandia (Author), Matt Pepe (Author) "Truth is stranger than fiction..." (more)
- Ross, S. and Gow, A. (1999). *Digital archaeology? Rescuing Neglected or Damaged Data Resources* (PDF). Bristol & London: British Library and Joint Information Systems Committee. ISBN 1-900508-51-6.
- George M. Mohay (2003). *Computer and intrusion forensics*. Artech House. p. 395. ISBN 1-58053-369-8.
- Chuck Easttom (2013). *System Forensics, Investigation, and Response*. Jones & Bartlett. p. 318. ISBN 1284031055.

1.7.1 Related journals

- *IEEE Transactions on Information Forensics and Security*
- *Journal of Digital Forensics, Security and Law*
- *International Journal of Digital Crime and Forensics*
- *Journal of Digital Investigation*
- *International Journal of Digital Evidence*
- *International Journal of Forensic Computer Science*
- *Journal of Digital Forensic Practice*
- *Cryptologia*
- *Small Scale Digital Device Forensic Journal*

1.8 External links

- US NIST Digital Data Acquisition Tool Specification (PDF)

- Forensics Wiki, a Creative Commons wiki of computer forensics information.

- Computer Forensics World Forum

- Original Computer Forensics Wiki

- Electronic Evidence Information Center

- Forensic Focus

- Digital Forensic Research Workshop (DFRWS)

- Computer Forensic Whitepapers (SANS)

Chapter 2

Indicator of compromise

Indicator of compromise (IOC) — in computer forensics is an artifact observed on a network or in an operating system that with high confidence indicates a computer intrusion.[1]

Typical IOCs are virus signatures and IP addresses, MD5 hashes of malware files or URLs or domain names of botnet command and control servers. After IOCs have been identified in a process of incident response and computer forensics, they can be used for early detection of future attack attempts using intrusion detection systems and antivirus software.

For more efficient automated processing there are initiatives to standardize format of IOCs.[2][3] Known indicators are usually exchanged within the industry.[4]

2.1 References

[1] "Understanding Indicators of Compromise (IOC) Part I". RSA. 2012. Retrieved February 27, 2013.

[2] "The Incident Object Description Exchange Format". *RFC 5070*. IETF. 2007. Retrieved February 27, 2013.

[3] "Cyber Observable eXpression (CybOX)". Mitre. Retrieved February 27, 2013.

[4] "IOC Bucket".

Chapter 3

Anti-computer forensics

Anti-computer forensics (sometimes **counter forensics**) is a general term for a set of techniques used as countermeasures to forensic analysis.

3.1 Definition

Anti-forensics has only recently been recognized as a legitimate field of study. Within this field of study, numerous definitions of anti-forensics abound. One of the more widely known and accepted definitions comes from Dr. Marc Rogers of Purdue University. Dr. Rogers uses a more traditional "crime scene" approach when defining anti-forensics. "Attempts to negatively affect the existence, amount and/or quality of evidence from a crime scene, or make the analysis and examination of evidence difficult or impossible to conduct."[1]

A more abbreviated definition is given by Scott Berinato in his article entitled, The Rise of Anti-Forensics. "Anti-forensics is more than technology. It is an approach to criminal hacking that can be summed up like this: Make it hard for them to find you and impossible for them to prove they found you."[2] Neither author takes into account using anti-forensics methods to ensure the privacy of one's personal data.

3.1.1 Sub-categories

Anti-forensics methods are often broken down into several sub-categories to make classification of the various tools and techniques simpler. One of the more widely accepted subcategory breakdowns was developed by Dr. Marcus Rogers. He has proposed the following sub-categories: data hiding, artifact wiping, trail obfuscation and attacks against the CF (computer forensics) processes and tools.[1] Attacks against forensics tools directly has also been called counter-forensics.[3]

3.1.2 Purpose and goals

Within the field of digital forensics there is much debate over the purpose and goals of anti-forensic methods. The common conception is that anti-forensic tools are purely malicious in intent and design. Others believe that these tools should be used to illustrate deficiencies in digital forensic procedures, digital forensic tools, and forensic examiner education. This sentiment was echoed at the 2005 Blackhat Conference by anti-forensic tool authors, James Foster and Vinnie Liu.[4] They stated that by exposing these issues, forensic investigators will have to work harder to prove that collected evidence is both accurate and dependable. They believe that this will result in better tools and education for the forensic examiner. Also, counter-forensics has significance for defence against espionage, as recovering information by forensic tools serves the goals of spies equally as well as investigators.

3.2 Data hiding

Data hiding is the process of making data difficult to find while also keeping it accessible for future use. "Obfuscation and encryption of data give an adversary the ability to limit identification and collection of evidence by investigators while allowing access and use to themselves."[5]

Some of the more common forms of data hiding include encryption, steganography and other various forms of hardware/software based data concealment. Each of the different data hiding methods makes digital forensic examinations difficult. When the different data hiding methods are combined, they can make a successful forensic investigation nearly impossible.

3.2.1 Encryption

One of the more commonly used techniques to defeat computer forensics is data encryption. In a presentation he gave on encryption and anti-forensic methodologies the Vice President of Secure Computing, Paul Henry, referred to encryption as a "forensic expert's nightmare".[6]

The majority of publicly available encryption programs allow the user to create virtual encrypted disks which can only be opened with a designated key. Through the use of modern encryption algorithms and various encryption techniques these programs make the data virtually impossible to read without the designated key.

File level encryption encrypts only the file contents. This leaves important information such as file name, size and timestamps unencrypted. Parts of the content of the file can be reconstructed from other locations, such as temporary files, swap file and deleted, unencrypted copies.

Most encryption programs have the ability to perform a number of additional functions that make digital forensic efforts increasingly difficult. Some of these functions include the use of a keyfile, full-volume encryption, and plausible deniability. The widespread availability of software containing these functions has put the field of digital forensics at a great disadvantage.

3.2.2 Steganography

Steganography is a technique where information or files are hidden within another file in an attempt to hide data by leaving it in plain sight. "Steganography produces dark data that is typically buried within light data (e.g., a non-perceptible digital watermark buried within a digital photograph)."[7] Some experts have argued that the use of steganography techniques are not very widespread and therefore shouldn't be given a lot of thought. Most experts will agree that steganography has the capability of disrupting the forensic process when used correctly.[2]

According to Jeffrey Carr, a 2007 edition of Technical Mujahid (a bi-monthly terrorist publication) outlined the importance of using a steganography program called Secrets of the Mujahideen. According to Carr, the program was touted as giving the user the capability to avoid detection by current steganalysis programs. It did this through the use of steganography in conjunction with file compression.[8]

3.2.3 Other forms of data hiding

Other forms of data hiding involve the use of tools and techniques to hide data throughout various locations in a computer system. Some of these places can include "memory, slack space, hidden directories, bad blocks, alternate data streams, (and) hidden partitions."[1]

One of the more well known tools that is often used

for data hiding is called Slacker (part of the Metasploit framework).[9] Slacker breaks up a file and places each piece of that file into the slack space of other files, thereby hiding it from the forensic examination software.[7] Another data hiding technique involves the use of bad sectors. To perform this technique, the user changes a particular sector from good to bad and then data is placed onto that particular cluster. The belief is that forensic examination tools will see these clusters as bad and continue on without any examination of their contents.[7]

3.3 Artifact wiping

See also: Data erasure

The methods used in artifact wiping are tasked with permanently eliminating particular files or entire file systems. This can be accomplished through the use of a variety of methods that include disk cleaning utilities, file wiping utilities and disk degaussing/destruction techniques.[1]

3.3.1 Disk cleaning utilities

Disk cleaning utilities use a variety of methods to overwrite the existing data on disks (see data remanence). The effectiveness of disk cleaning utilities as anti-forensic tools is often challenged as some believe they are not completely effective. Experts who don't believe that disk cleaning utilities are acceptable for disk sanitization base their opinions of current DOD policy, which states that the only acceptable form of sanitization is degaussing. (See National Industrial Security Program.) Disk cleaning utilities are also criticized because they leave signatures that the file system was wiped, which in some cases is unacceptable. Some of the widely used disk cleaning utilities include DBAN, srm, BCWipe Total WipeOut, KillDisk, PC Inspector and CyberScrubs cyberCide. Another option which is approved by the NIST and the NSA is CMRR Secure Erase, which uses the Secure Erase command built into the ATA specification.

3.3.2 File wiping utilities

File wiping utilities are used to delete individual files from an operating system. The advantage of file wiping utilities is that they can accomplish their task in a relatively short amount of time as opposed to disk cleaning utilities which take much longer. Another advantage of file wiping utilities is that they generally leave a much smaller signature than disk cleaning utilities. There are two primary disadvantages of file wiping utilities, first they require user involvement in the process and second some experts believe that file wiping programs don't always correctly and completely wipe file information.[1] Some of the widely used file wiping utilities include BCWipe, R-Wipe & Clean, Eraser, Aevita Wipe & Delete and CyberScrubs PrivacySuite.

3.3.3 Disk degaussing / destruction techniques

Disk degaussing is a process by which a magnetic field is applied to a digital media device. The result is a device that is entirely clean of any previously stored data. Degaussing is rarely used as an anti-forensic method despite the fact that it is an effective means to ensure data has been wiped. This is attributed to the high cost of degaussing machines, which are difficult for the average consumer to afford.

A more commonly used technique to ensure data wiping is the physical destruction of the device. The NIST recommends that "physical destruction can be accomplished using a variety of methods, including disintegration, incineration, pulverizing, shredding and melting."[10]

3.4 Trail obfuscation

The purpose of trail obfuscation is to confuse, disorient, and divert the forensic examination process. Trail obfuscation covers a variety of techniques and tools that include "log cleaners, spoofing, misinformation, backbone hopping, zombied accounts, trojan commands."[1]

One of the more widely known trail obfuscation tools is Timestomp (part of the Metasploit Framework).[9] Timestomp gives the user the ability to modify file metadata pertaining to access, creation and modification times/dates.[2] By using programs such as Timestomp, a user can render any number of files useless in a legal setting by directly calling into question the files' credibility.

Another well known trail-obfuscation program is Transmogrify (also part of the Metasploit Framework).[9] In most file types the header of the file contains identifying information. A (.jpg) would have header information that identifies it as a (.jpg), a (.doc) would have information that identifies it as (.doc) and so on. Transmogrify allows the user to change the header information of a file, so a (.jpg) header could be changed to a (.doc) header. If a forensic examination program or operating system were to conduct a search for images on a machine, it would simply see a (.doc) file and skip over it.[2]

3.5 Attacks against computer forensics

In the past anti-forensic tools have focused on attacking the forensic process by destroying data, hiding data, or altering data usage information. Anti-forensics has recently moved into a new realm where tools and techniques are focused on attacking forensic tools that perform the examinations. These new anti-forensic methods have benefited from a number of factors to include well documented forensic examination procedures, widely known forensic tool vulnerabilities and digital forensic examiners heavy reliance on their tools.[1]

During a typical forensic examination, the examiner would create an image of the computer's disks. This keeps the original computer (evidence) from being tainted by forensic tools. Hashes are created by the forensic examination software to verify the integrity of the image. One of the recent anti-tool techniques targets the integrity of the hash that is created to verify the image. By affecting the integrity of the hash, any evidence that is collected during the subsequent investigation can be challenged.[1]

3.6 Physical

Use of chassis intrusion detection feature in computer case or a sensor (such as a photodetector) rigged with explosives for self-destruction.

3.7 Effectiveness of anti-forensics

Anti-forensic methods rely on several weaknesses in the forensic process including: the human element, dependency on tools, and the physical/logical limitations of computers.[11] By reducing the forensic process's susceptibility to these weaknesses, an examiner can reduce the likelihood of anti-forensic methods successfully impacting an investigation.[11] This may be accomplished by providing increased training for investigators, and corroborating results using multiple tools.

3.8 Notes and references

[1] Rogers, D. M. (2005). Anti-Forensic Presentation given to Lockheed Martin. San Diego.

[2] Berinato, S. (2007). The Rise of Anti Forensics. Retrieved April 19, 2008, from CSO Online: http://www.csoonline.com/article/221208/The_Rise_of_Anti_Forensics

[3] Hartley, W. Matthew. (2007). Current and Future Threats to Digital Forensics. https://www.issa.org/ Library/Journals/2007/August/Hartley-Current%20and% 20Future%20Threats%20to%20Digital%20Forensics.pdf

[4] "Black Hat USA 2005 – Catch Me If You Can – 27July2005". Foster, J. C., & Liu, V. (2005). Retrieved 11 January 2016.

[5] Peron, C.S.J. (n.a.). Digital anti-forensics: Emerging trends in data transformation techniques. from Seccuris: http://www.seccuris.com/documents/whitepapers/ Seccuris-Antiforensics.pdf

[6] Henry, P. A. (2006). *Secure Computing with Anti-Forensics* [LayerOne video file]. Retrieved from http://www.youtube. com/watch?v=q9VUbiFdx7w&t=2m18s

[7] Berghel, H. (2007 / Vol. 50, No. 4). Hiding Data, Forensics, and Anti-Forensics. Communications of the ACM , 15-20.

[8] Carr, J. (2007). Anti-Forensic Methods Used by Jihadist Web Sites. Retrieved April 21, 2008, from eSecurity-Planet: http://www.esecurityplanet.com/prevention/article. php/3694711

[9] "Metasploit Anti-Forensics Project (MAFIA) - Bishop Fox". Vincent Liu. Retrieved 11 January 2016.

[10] Kissel, R., Scholl, M., Skolochenko, S., & Li, X. (2006). Guidelines for Media Sanitization. Gaithersburg: Computer Security Division, National Institute of Standards and Technology.

[11] Harris, R. (2006). Arriving at an anti-forensics consensus: Examining how to define and control the anti-forensics problem. Retrieved December 9, 2010, from: http://www.dfrws. org/2006/proceedings/6-Harris.pdf

3.9   See also

- Forensic disk controller

- Data remanence

- Information privacy

- Cryptographic hash function

- Degauss

- Keyfile

- Encryption

- Plausible deniability

- Metadata removal tool

- DECAF

3.10   External links

- Evaluating Commercial Counter-Forensic Tools

- Counter-Forensic Tools: Analysis and Data Recovery

- http://www.informatik.uni-trier.de/~{ }ley/db/conf/ dfrws/dfrws2005.html

- http://www.dfrws.org/2006/proceedings/6-Harris. pdf

- Anti-Forensics Class Little over 3hr of video on the subject of anti-forensic techniques

Chapter 4

Anubisnetworks

Warning: Page using Template:Infobox company with unknown parameter "company TM" (this message is shown only in preview).
Warning: Page using Template:Infobox company with unknown parameter "presence" (this message is shown only in preview).
Warning: Page using Template:Infobox company with unknown parameter "Office locations" (this message is shown only in preview).

AnubisNetworks is a cybersecurity/ Threat Intelligence IT company, best known for its Real-time Threat Intelligence offer, Cyberfeed. Cyberfeed is a subscription based service that allows customers to obtain real time intelligence feeds about events related to security threats, as seen worldwide, with relevance to their organization. Mail Protection Service (MPS) portfolio represent another important product line and it comprises a set of customized solutions for managing and filtering messaging traffic in a Multitenancy environment.

4.1 History

Founded in 2006 by experts of the corporate Telecom industry, AnubisNetworks is currently one of Europe´s leading Threat Intelligence and Email Security suppliers. Some of worlds' largest providers (for instance: Vodafone, BT) use AnubisNetworks' technology.

In June 2014, AnubisNetworks Threat Intelligence solution, Cyberfeed, was part of Operation Tovar which resulted in the takedown of Gameover ZeuS botnet.

On the 21st of October 2014 it was announced that Anubis-Networks was acquired by BitSight Technologies, the leading provider of information security ratings for organizations around the world.[1]

4.2 See also

- Computer security
- Countermeasure (computer)
- IT risk
- Threat (computer)

4.3 References

[1] http://bitsig.ht/1ybf9hQ

- Bitsight announcement
- Virus bulletin profile
- Official Release of US Dept. of Justice
- 451Research report on AnubisNetworks
- BitSight acquisition announcement

4.4 External links

- Official website
- BitSight Technologies website
- AnubisNetworks' contacts
- Proprietary reputation technology
- Spam Monitor for Twitter Feeds
- Live Global Botnet visualizer

Chapter 5

Autopsy (software)

Autopsy is a user interface that makes it simpler to deploy many of the open source programs and plugins used in the Sleuth Kit collection.[1] The graphical user interface displays the results from the forensic search of the underlying volume making it easier for investigators to flag pertinent sections of the data. The tool is largely maintained by Basis Technology Corp. with the assistance of programmers throughout the community. The company sells support services and training for using the product.[2]

The tool is designed with these principles in mind:

- *Extensible*—The user should be able to add new functionality by creating plugins that can analyze all or part of the underlying data source.

- *Frameworks*—The tool will offer some standard approaches for ingesting data, analyzing it and reporting any findings so developers can follow the same design patterns when possible.

- *Ease of Use*—The Autopsy Browser must offer the wizards and historical tools to make it easier for users to repeat their steps without excessive reconfiguration.

The core browser can be extended by adding modules that help scan the files (called "ingesting"), browse the results (called "viewing") or summarize results (called "reporting"). A collection of open-source modules allow customization.

Version 2 of Autopsy is written in Perl and it runs on all major platforms including Linux, Unix, Mac OS X, and Windows. It relies upon the Sleuth Kit to analyze the disk. Version 2 is released under the GNU GPL 2.0.[3]

Autopsy 3.0 is written in Java using the NetBeans platform. It runs only on Windows at this time and is released under the Apache license 2.0.[3]

Autopsy depends on a number of libraries with various licenses.[3]

5.1 References

[1] Sleuth Kit site

[2] Basis Technology site

[3] http://www.sleuthkit.org/autopsy/licenses.php

5.2 External links

- Autopsy Page
- The Sleuth Kit Official website
- The Sleuth Kit Informer newsletter
- Sleuth Kit Wiki

Chapter 6

Certified Computer Examiner

The **Certified Computer Examiner** (**CCE**) credential demonstrates competency in computer forensics. The CCE is offered by the International Society for Computer Examiners (ISFCE), an organization that hopes to create and maintain high standards for computer examiners worldwide.

6.1 Qualifications

Candidates for the CCE must have no criminal record and adhere to the ISFCE code of ethics. They should have at least 18 months of professional experience or documented training, and pass an online examination. As well as the online examination, candidates must perform a forensic examination on at least three "test media".

Once candidates have successfully completed the requirements of the ISFCE, they are considered Certified Computer Examiners and members of the ISFCE.

To maintain the credential of Certified Computer Examiner, fifty hours of education or training must be completed every two years. In addition, candidates must work on at least three media during that period. An online examination is also required every two years for recertification.

6.2 External links

- Official website

Chapter 7

Computer and network surveillance

This article is about monitoring of computer and network activity. For information on methods of preventing unauthorized access to computer data, see computer security.
Main article: Surveillance

Computer and network surveillance is the monitoring of computer activity and data stored on a hard drive, or data being transferred over computer networks such as the Internet. The monitoring is often carried out covertly and may be completed by governments, corporations, criminal organizations, or individuals. It may or may not be legal and may or may not require authorization from a court or other independent government agency.

Computer and network surveillance programs are widespread today and almost all Internet traffic can be monitored for illegal activity.[1]

Surveillance allows governments and other agencies to maintain social control, recognize and monitor threats, and prevent and investigate criminal activity. With the advent of programs such as the Total Information Awareness program, technologies such as high speed surveillance computers and biometrics software, and laws such as the Communications Assistance For Law Enforcement Act, governments now possess an unprecedented ability to monitor the activities of citizens.[2]

However, many civil rights and privacy groups, such as Reporters Without Borders, the Electronic Frontier Foundation, and the American Civil Liberties Union, have expressed concern that with increasing surveillance of citizens we will end up in or are even already in a mass surveillance society, with limited political and/or personal freedoms. Such fear has led to numerous lawsuits such as *Hepting v. AT&T*.[2][3] The hacktivist group Anonymous has hacked into government websites in protest of what it considers "draconian surveillance".[4][5]

7.1 Network surveillance

See also: Signals intelligence

The vast majority of computer surveillance involves the monitoring of data and traffic on the Internet.[6] For example, in the United States, the Communications Assistance For Law Enforcement Act, mandates that all phone calls and broadband internet traffic (emails, web traffic, instant messaging, etc.) be available for unimpeded, real-time monitoring by Federal law enforcement agencies.[7][8][9]

Packet capture (also known as "packet sniffing") is the monitoring of data traffic on a computer network.[10] Data sent between computers over the Internet or between any networks takes the form of small chunks called packets, which are routed to their destination and assembled back into a complete message. A Packet Capture Appliance intercepts these packets, so that they may be examined and analyzed. Computer technology is needed to perform traffic analysis and sift through intercepted data to look for important/useful information. Under the Communications Assistance For Law Enforcement Act, all U.S. telecommunications providers are required to install such packet capture technology so that Federal law enforcement and intelligence agencies are able to intercept all of their customers' broadband Internet and voice over Internet protocol (VoIP) traffic.[11]

There is far too much data gathered by these packet sniffers for human investigators to manually search through. Thus, automated Internet surveillance computers sift through the vast amount of intercepted Internet traffic, filtering out, and reporting to investigators those bits of information which are "interesting", for example, the use of certain words or phrases, visiting certain types of web sites, or communicating via email or chat with a certain individual or group.[12] Billions of dollars per year are spent by agencies such as the Information Awareness Office, NSA, and the FBI, for the development, purchase, implementation, and operation of systems which intercept and analyze this data, extracting only the information that is useful to law enforcement and intelligence agencies.[13]

Similar systems are now used by Iranian secret police to identify and suppress dissidents. All of the technology has been allegedly installed by German Siemens AG and Finnish Nokia.[14]

The Internet's rapid development has become a primary form of communication. More people are potentially subject to Internet surveillance. There are advantages and disadvantages to network monitoring. For instance, systems described as "Web 2.0"[15] have greatly impacted modern society. An advantage to online surveillance is that large social media platforms, such as YouTube, Twitter and Facebook, enable people to contact friends, family, and strangers daily. Tim O' Reilly, who first explained the concept of "Web 2.0",[15] stated that Web 2.0 provides communication platforms that are "user generated", with self-produced content, motivating more people to communicate with friends online.[16] However, Internet surveillance also has a disadvantage. One researcher from Uppsala University said "Web 2.0 surveillance is directed at large user groups who help to hegemonically produce and reproduce surveillance by providing user-generated (self-produced) content. We can characterize Web 2.0 surveillance as mass self-surveillance".[17] Surveillance companies monitor people while they are focused on work or entertainment. This can emotionally affect people; this is because it can cause emotions like jealousy. A research group states "...we set out to test the prediction that feelings of jealousy lead to 'creeping' on a partner through Facebook, and that women are particularly likely to engage in partner monitoring in response to jealousy".[18] The study shows that women can become jealous of other people when they are in an online group.

7.2 Corporate surveillance

See also: Computer surveillance in the workplace

Corporate surveillance of computer activity is very common. The data collected is most often used for marketing purposes or sold to other corporations, but is also regularly shared with government agencies. It can be used as a form of business intelligence, which enables the corporation to better tailor their products and/or services to be desirable by their customers. Or the data can be sold to other corporations, so that they can use it for the aforementioned purpose. Or it can be used for direct marketing purposes, such as targeted advertisements, where ads are targeted to the user of the search engine by analyzing their search history and emails[19] (if they use free webmail services), which is kept in a database.[20]

One important component of prevention is establishing the business purposes of monitoring, which may include the following: Preventing misuse of resources. Companies can discourage unproductive personal activities such as online shopping or web surfing on company time. Monitoring employee performance is one way to reduce unnecessary network traffic and reduce the consumption of network bandwidth. Promoting adherence to policies. Online surveillance is one means of verifying employee observance of company networking policies. Preventing lawsuits. Firms can be held liable for discrimination or employee harassment in the workplace. Organizations can also be involved in infringement suits through employees that distribute copyrighted material over corporate networks. Safeguarding records. Federal legislation requires organizations to protect personal information. Monitoring can determine the extent of compliance with company policies and programs overseeing information security. Monitoring may also deter unlawful appropriation of personal information, and potential spam or viruses. Safeguarding company assets. The protection of intellectual property, trade secrets, and business strategies is a major concern. The ease of information transmission and storage makes it imperative to monitor employee actions as part of a broader policy. A second component of prevention is determining the ownership of technology resources. The ownership of the firm's networks, servers, computers, files, and e-mail should be explicitly stated. There should be a distinction between an employee's personal electronic devices, which should be limited and proscribed, and those owned by the firm.

For instance, Google, the world's most popular search engine, stores identifying information for each web search. An IP address and the search phrase used are stored in a database for up to 18 months.[21] Google also scans the content of emails of users of its Gmail webmail service, in order to create targeted advertising based on what people are talking about in their personal email correspondences.[22] Google is, by far, the largest Internet advertising agency— millions of sites place Google's advertising banners and links on their websites, in order to earn money from visitors who click on the ads. Each page containing Google advertisements adds, reads, and modifies "cookies" on each visitor's computer.[23] These cookies track the user across all of these sites, and gather information about their web surfing habits, keeping track of which sites they visit, and what they do when they are on these sites. This information, along with the information from their email accounts, and search engine histories, is stored by Google to use to build a profile of the user to deliver better-targeted advertising.[22]

The United States government often gains access to these databases, either by producing a warrant for it, or by simply asking. The Department of Homeland Security has openly stated that it uses data collected from consumer credit and direct marketing agencies for augmenting the profiles of individuals that it is monitoring.[20]

7.3 Malicious software

Further information: Spyware, Computer virus, Trojan (computer security), Keylogger and Backdoor (computing)

In addition to monitoring information sent over a computer network, there is also a way to examine data stored on a computer's hard drive, and to monitor the activities of a person using the computer. A surveillance program installed on a computer can search the contents of the hard drive for suspicious data, can monitor computer use, collect passwords, and/or report back activities in real-time to its operator through the Internet connection.[24] Keylogger is an example of this type of program. Normal keylogging programs store their data on the local hard drive, but some are programmed to automatically transmit data over the network to a remote computer or Web server.

There are multiple ways of installing such software. The most common is remote installation, using a backdoor created by a computer virus or trojan. This tactic has the advantage of potentially subjecting multiple computers to surveillance. Viruses often spread to thousands or millions of computers, and leave "backdoors" which are accessible over a network connection, and enable an intruder to remotely install software and execute commands. These viruses and trojans are sometimes developed by government agencies, such as CIPAV and Magic Lantern. More often, however, viruses created by other people or spyware installed by marketing agencies can be used to gain access through the security breaches that they create.[25]

Another method is "cracking" into the computer to gain access over a network. An attacker can then install surveillance software remotely. Servers and computers with permanent broadband connections are most vulnerable to this type of attack.[26] Another source of security cracking is employees giving out information or users using brute force tactics to guess their password.[27]

One can also physically place surveillance software on a computer by gaining entry to the place where the computer is stored and install it from a compact disc, floppy disk, or thumbdrive. This method shares a disadvantage with hardware devices in that it requires physical access to the computer.[28] One well-known worm that uses this method of spreading itself is Stuxnet.[29]

7.4 Social network analysis

One common form of surveillance is to create maps of social networks based on data from social networking sites as well as from traffic analysis information from phone call records such as those in the NSA call database,[30] and internet traffic data gathered under CALEA. These social network "maps" are then data mined to extract useful information such as personal interests, friendships and affiliations, wants, beliefs, thoughts, and activities.[31][32][33]

Many U.S. government agencies such as the Defense Advanced Research Projects Agency (DARPA), the National Security Agency (NSA), and the Department of Homeland Security (DHS) are currently investing heavily in research involving social network analysis.[34][35] The intelligence community believes that the biggest threat to the U.S. comes from decentralized, leaderless, geographically dispersed groups. These types of threats are most easily countered by finding important nodes in the network, and removing them. To do this requires a detailed map of the network.[33][36]

Jason Ethier of Northeastern University, in his study of modern social network analysis, said the following of the Scalable Social Network Analysis Program developed by the Information Awareness Office:

> The purpose of the SSNA algorithms program is to extend techniques of social network analysis to assist with distinguishing potential terrorist cells from legitimate groups of people ... In order to be successful SSNA will require information on the social interactions of the majority of people around the globe. Since the Defense Department cannot easily distinguish between peaceful citizens and terrorists, it will be necessary for them to gather data on innocent civilians as well as on potential terrorists.
>
> — Jason Ethier[33]

7.5 Monitoring from a distance

It has been shown that it is possible to monitor computers from a distance, with only commercially available equipment, by detecting the radiation emitted by the CRT monitor. This form of computer surveillance, known as TEMPEST, involves reading electromagnetic emanations from computing devices in order to extract data from them at distances of hundreds of meters.[37][38][39]

IBM researchers have also found that, for most computer keyboards, each key emits a slightly different noise when pressed. The differences are individually identifiable under some conditions, and so it's possible to log key strokes without actually requiring logging software to run on the associated computer.[40][41]

And it has also been shown, by Adi Shamir et al., that even the high frequency noise emitted by a CPU includes information about the instructions being executed.[42]

7.6 Policeware and govware

Policeware is software designed to police citizens by monitoring discussion and interaction of its citizens.[43] Within the U.S., Carnivore was a first incarnation of secretly installed e-mail monitoring software installed in Internet service providers' networks to log computer communication, including transmitted e-mails.[44] Magic Lantern is another such application, this time running in a targeted computer in a trojan style and performing keystroke logging. CIPAV, deployed by FBI, is a multi-purpose spyware/trojan.

The "Consumer Broadband and Digital Television Promotion Act" (CBDTA) was a bill proposed in the United States Congress. CBDTPA was known as the "Security Systems and Standards Certification Act" (SSSCA) while in draft form, and was killed in committee in 2002. Had CBDTPA become law, it would have prohibited technology that could be used to read digital content under copyright (such as music, video, and e-books) without Digital Rights Management (DRM) that prevented access to this material without the permission of the copyright holder.[45]

In German-speaking countries, spyware used or made by the government is sometimes called *govware*.[46] Some countries like Switzerland and Germany have a legal framework governing the use of such software.[47][48] Known examples include the Swiss MiniPanzer and MegaPanzer and the German R2D2 (trojan).

7.7 Surveillance as an aid to censorship

See also: Internet censorship and Internet censorship circumvention

Surveillance and censorship are different. Surveillance can be performed without censorship, but it is harder to engage in censorship without some form of surveillance.[49] And even when surveillance does not lead directly to censorship, the widespread knowledge or belief that a person, their computer, or their use of the Internet is under surveillance can lead to self-censorship.[50]

In March 2013 Reporters Without Borders issued a *Special report on Internet surveillance* that examines the use of technology that monitors online activity and intercepts electronic communication in order to arrest journalists, citizen-journalists, and dissidents. The report includes a list of "State Enemies of the Internet", Bahrain, China, Iran, Syria, and Vietnam, countries whose governments are involved in active, intrusive surveillance of news providers, resulting in grave violations of freedom of information and human rights. Computer and network surveillance is on the increase in these countries. The report also includes a second list of "Corporate Enemies of the Internet", Amesys (France), Blue Coat Systems (U.S.), Gamma (UK and Germany), Hacking Team (Italy), and Trovicor (Germany), companies that sell products that are liable to be used by governments to violate human rights and freedom of information. Neither list is exhaustive and they are likely to be expanded in the future.[51]

Protection of sources is no longer just a matter of journalistic ethics. Journalists should equip themselves with a "digital survival kit" if they are exchanging sensitive information online, storing it on a computer hard-drive or mobile phone.[51][52] Individuals associated with high profile rights organizations, dissident groups, protest groups, or reform groups are urged to take extra precautions to protect their online identities.[53]

7.8 See also

- Anonymizer, a software system that attempts to make network activity untraceable

- Computer surveillance in the workplace

- Cyber spying

- Differential privacy, a method to maximize the accuracy of queries from statistical databases while minimizing the chances of violating the privacy of individuals.

- ECHELON, a signals intelligence (SIGINT) collection and analysis network operated on behalf of Australia, Canada, New Zealand, the United Kingdom, and the United States, also known as AUSCANNZUKUS and Five Eyes

- GhostNet, a large-scale cyber spying operation discovered in March 2009

- List of government surveillance projects

- Mass surveillance
  - China's Golden Shield Project

- Mass surveillance in Australia
- Mass surveillance in China
- Mass surveillance in East Germany
- Mass surveillance in India
- Mass surveillance in North Korea
- Mass surveillance in the United Kingdom
- Mass surveillance in the United States

- Surveillance

- Surveillance by the United States government:

  - 2013 mass surveillance disclosures, reports about NSA and its international partners' mass surveillance of foreign nationals and U.S. citizens
  - Bullrun (code name), a highly classified NSA program to preserve its ability to eavesdrop on encrypted communications by influencing and weakening encryption standards, by obtaining master encryption keys, and by gaining access to data before or after it is encrypted either by agreement, by force of law, or by computer network exploitation (hacking)
  - Carnivore, a U.S. Federal Bureau of Investigation system to monitor email and electronic communications
  - COINTELPRO, a series of covert, and at times illegal, projects conducted by the FBI aimed at U.S. domestic political organizations
  - Communications Assistance For Law Enforcement Act
  - Computer and Internet Protocol Address Verifier (CIPAV), a data gathering tool used by the U.S. Federal Bureau of Investigation (FBI)
  - Dropmire, a secret surveillance program by the NSA aimed at surveillance of foreign embassies and diplomatic staff, including those of NATO allies
  - Magic Lantern, keystroke logging software developed by the U.S. Federal Bureau of Investigation
  - Mass surveillance in the United States
  - NSA call database, a database containing metadata for hundreds of billions of telephone calls made in the U.S.
  - NSA warrantless surveillance (2001–07)
  - NSA whistleblowers: William Binney, Thomas Andrews Drake, Mark Klein, Edward Snowden, Thomas Tamm, Russ Tice

- Spying on United Nations leaders by United States diplomats
- Stellar Wind (code name), code name for information collected under the President's Surveillance Program
- Tailored Access Operations, NSA's hacking program
- Terrorist Surveillance Program, an NSA electronic surveillance program
- Total Information Awareness, a project of the Defense Advanced Research Projects Agency (DARPA)

- TEMPEST, codename for studies of unintentional intelligence-bearing signals which, if intercepted and analyzed, may disclose the information transmitted, received, handled, or otherwise processed by any information-processing equipment

7.9 References

[1] Anne Broache. "FBI wants widespread monitoring of 'illegal' Internet activity". *CNET*. Retrieved 25 March 2014.

[2] "Is the U.S. Turning Into a Surveillance Society?". *American Civil Liberties Union*. Retrieved March 13, 2009.

[3] "Bigger Monster, Weaker Chains: The Growth of an American Surveillance Society" (PDF). *American Civil Liberties Union*. January 15, 2003. Retrieved March 13, 2009.

[4] "Anonymous hacks UK government sites over 'draconian surveillance' ", Emil Protalinski, ZDNet, 7 April 2012, retrieved 12 March 2013

[5] Hacktivists in the frontline battle for the internet retrieved 17 June 2012

[6] Diffie, Whitfield; Susan Landau (August 2008). "Internet Eavesdropping: A Brave New World of Wiretapping". *Scientific American*. Retrieved 2009-03-13.

[7] "CALEA Archive -- Electronic Frontier Foundation". *Electronic Frontier Foundation (website)*. Retrieved 2009-03-14.

[8] "CALEA: The Perils of Wiretapping the Internet". *Electronic Frontier Foundation (website)*. Retrieved 2009-03-14.

[9] "CALEA: Frequently Asked Questions". *Electronic Frontier Foundation (website)*. Retrieved 2009-03-14.

[10] Kevin J. Connolly (2003). *Law of Internet Security and Privacy*. Aspen Publishers. p. 131. ISBN 978-0-7355-4273-0.

[11] American Council on Education vs. FCC, Decision, United States Court of Appeals for the District of Columbia Circuit, 9 June 2006. Retrieved 8 September 2013.

[12] Hill, Michael (October 11, 2004). "Government funds chat room surveillance research". USA Today. Associated Press. Retrieved 2009-03-19.

[13] McCullagh, Declan (January 30, 2007). "FBI turns to broad new wiretap method". *ZDNet News*. Retrieved 2009-03-13.

[14] "First round in Internet war goes to Iranian intelligence", Debkafile, 28 June 2009. (subscription required)

[15] O'Reilly, T. (2005). What is Web 2.0: Design Patterns and Business Models for the Next Generation of Software. O'Reilly Media, 1-5.

[16] Fuchs, C. (2011). New Media, Web 2.0 and Surveillance. Sociology Compass, 134-147.

[17] Fuchs, C. (2011). Web 2.0, Presumption, and Surveillance. Surveillance & Society, 289-309.

[18] Muise, A., Christofides, E., & Demsmarais, S. (2014). "Creeping" or just information seeking? Gender differences in partner monitoring in response to jealousy on Facebook. Personal Relationships, 21(1), 35-50.

[19] Story, Louise (November 1, 2007). "F.T.C. to Review Online Ads and Privacy". *New York Times*. Retrieved 2009-03-17.

[20] Butler, Don (January 31, 2009). "Are we addicted to being watched?". *The Ottawa Citizen* (canada.com). Retrieved 26 May 2013.

[21] Soghoian, Chris (September 11, 2008). "Debunking Google's log anonymization propaganda". *CNET News*. Retrieved 2009-03-21.

[22] Joshi, Priyanki (March 21, 2009). "Every move you make, Google will be watching you". *Business Standard*. Retrieved 2009-03-21.

[23] "Advertising and Privacy". *Google (company page)*. 2009. Retrieved 2009-03-21.

[24] "Spyware Workshop: Monitoring Software on Your OC: Spywae, Adware, and Other Software", Staff Report, U.S. Federal Trade Commission, March 2005. Retrieved 7 September 2013.

[25] Aycock, John (2006). *Computer Viruses and Malware*. Springer. ISBN 978-0-387-30236-2.

[26] "Office workers give away passwords for a cheap pen", John Leyden, *The Register*, 8 April 2003. Retrieved 7 September 2013.

[27] "Passwords are passport to theft", *The Register*, 3 March 2004. Retrieved 7 September 2013.

[28] "Social Engineering Fundamentals, Part I: Hacker Tactics", Sarah Granger, 18 December 2001.

[29] "Stuxnet: How does the Stuxnet worm spread?". Antivirus.about.com. 2014-03-03. Retrieved 2014-05-17.

[30] Keefe, Patrick (March 12, 2006). "Can Network Theory Thwart Terrorists?". *New York Times*. Retrieved 14 March 2009.

[31] Albrechtslund, Anders (March 3, 2008). "Online Social Networking as Participatory Surveillance". *First Monday* **13** (3). Retrieved March 14, 2009.

[32] Fuchs, Christian (2009). *Social Networking Sites and the Surveillance Society. A Critical Case Study of the Usage of studiVZ, Facebook, and MySpace by Students in Salzburg in the Context of Electronic Surveillance* (PDF). Salzburg and Vienna: Forschungsgruppe Unified Theory of Information. ISBN 978-3-200-01428-2. Retrieved March 14, 2009.

[33] Ethier, Jason (27 May 2006). "Current Research in Social Network Theory" (PDF). Northeastern University College of Computer and Information Science. Retrieved 15 March 2009.

[34] Marks, Paul (June 9, 2006). "Pentagon sets its sights on social networking websites". *New Scientist*. Retrieved 2009-03-16.

[35] Kawamoto, Dawn (June 9, 2006). "Is the NSA reading your MySpace profile?". *CNET News*. Retrieved 2009-03-16.

[36] Ressler, Steve (July 2006). "Social Network Analysis as an Approach to Combat Terrorism: Past, Present, and Future Research". *Homeland Security Affairs* **II** (2). Retrieved March 14, 2009.

[37] McNamara, Joel (4 December 1999). "Complete, Unofficial Tempest Page". Retrieved 7 September 2013.

[38] Van Eck, Wim (1985). "Electromagnetic Radiation from Video Display Units: An Eavesdropping Risk?" (PDF). *Computers & Security* **4**: 269–286. doi:10.1016/0167-4048(85)90046-X.

[39] Kuhn, M.G. (26–28 May 2004). "Electromagnetic Eavesdropping Risks of Flat-Panel Displays" (PDF). *4th Workshop on Privacy Enhancing Technologies* (Toronto): 23–25.

[40] Asonov, Dmitri; Agrawal, Rakesh (2004), *Keyboard Acoustic Emanations* (PDF), IBM Almaden Research Center

[41] Yang, Sarah (14 September 2005), "Researchers recover typed text using audio recording of keystrokes", *UC Berkeley News*

[42] Adi Shamir & Eran Tromer. "Acoustic cryptanalysis". Blavatnik School of Computer Science, Tel Aviv University. Retrieved 1 November 2011.

[43] Jeremy Reimer (20 July 2007). "The tricky issue of spyware with a badge: meet 'policeware'". Ars Technica.

[44] Hopper, D. Ian (4 May 2001). "FBI's Web Monitoring Exposed". ABC News.

[45] "Consumer Broadband and Digital Television Promotion Act", U.S. Senate bill S.2048, 107th Congress, 2nd session, 21 March 2002. Retrieved 8 September 2013.

[46] "Swiss coder publicises government spy Trojan". News.techworld.com. Retrieved 25 March 2014.

[47] Basil Cupa, Trojan Horse Resurrected: On the Legality of the Use of Government Spyware (Govware), LISS 2013, pp. 419-428

[48] "FAQ – Häufig gestellte Fragen". Ejpd.admin.ch. 2011-11-23. Retrieved 2014-05-17.

[49] "Censorship is inseparable from surveillance", Cory Doctorow, *The Guardian*, 2 March 2012

[50] "Trends in transition from classical censorship to Internet censorship: selected country overviews"

[51] *The Enemies of the Internet Special Edition : Surveillance*, Reporters Without Borders, 12 March 2013

[52] "When Secrets Aren't Safe With Journalists", Christopher Soghoian, *New York Times*, 26 October 2011

[53] *Everyone's Guide to By-passing Internet Censorship*, The Citizen Lab, University of Toronto, September 2007

7.10   External links

- "Selected Papers in Anonymity", Free Haven Project, accessed 16 September 2011.

Chapter 8

Computer Online Forensic Evidence Extractor

Not to be confused with coffee.

Computer Online Forensic Evidence Extractor also said (**COFEE**) is a tool kit, developed by Microsoft, to help computer forensic investigators extract evidence from a Windows computer. Installed on a USB flash drive or other external disk drive, it acts as an automated forensic tool during a live analysis. Microsoft provides COFEE devices and online technical support free to law enforcement agencies.

8.1   Development and distribution

COFEE was developed by Anthony Fung, a former Hong Kong police officer who now works as a senior investigator on Microsoft's Internet Safety Enforcement Team.[1] Fung conceived the device following discussions he had at a 2006 law enforcement technology conference sponsored by Microsoft.[2] The device is used by more than 2,000 officers in at least 15 countries.[3]

A case cited by Microsoft in April 2008 credits COFEE as being crucial in a New Zealand investigation into the trafficking of child pornography, producing evidence that led to an arrest.[1]

In April 2009 Microsoft and Interpol signed an agreement under which INTERPOL would serve as principal international distributor of COFEE. University College Dublin's Center for Cyber Crime Investigations in conjunction with Interpol develops programs for training forensic experts in using COFEE.[4] The National White Collar Crime Center has been licensed by Microsoft to be the sole US domestic distributor of COFEE.[5]

8.1.1   Public leak

On November 6, 2009, copies of Microsoft COFEE were leaked onto various torrent websites.[6] Analysis of the leaked tool indicates that it is largely a wrapper around other utilities previously available to investigators.[7] Microsoft confirmed the leak; however a spokesperson for the firm said "We do not anticipate the possible availability of COFEE for cybercriminals to download and find ways to 'build around' to be a significant concern".[8]

8.2   Use

The device is activated by being plugged into a USB port. It contains 150 tools and a graphical user interface to help investigators collect data.[1] The software is reported to be made up of three sections. First COFEE is configured in advance with an investigator selecting the data they wish to export, this is then saved to a USB device for plugging into the target computer. A further interface generates reports from the collected data.[7] Estimates cited by Microsoft state jobs that previously took 3–4 hours can be done with COFEE in as little as 20 minutes.[1][9]

COFEE includes tools for password decryption, Internet history recovery and other data extraction.[2] It also recovers data stored in volatile memory which could be lost if the computer were shut down.[10]

8.3   DECAF

In mid to late 2009 a tool named Detect and Eliminate Computer Acquired Forensics (DECAF) was announced by an uninvolved group of programmers. The tool would reportedly protect computers against COFEE and render the tool ineffective.[11] It alleged that it would provide real-time monitoring of COFEE signatures on USB devices and in running applications and when a COFEE signature is detected, DECAF performs numerous user-defined processes. These included COFEE log clearing, ejecting USB devices, and contamination or spoofing of MAC addresses.[12] On December 18, 2009 the DECAF creators announced that the tool was a hoax and part of "a stunt to raise awareness for security and the need for better forensic tools".[13][14][15][16]

8.4 See also

- Kali Linux

- nUbuntu

- Windows To Go, bootable USB drive with Windows capable of running data recovery/collection utilities

8.5 References

[1] "Brad Smith: Law Enforcement Technology Conference 2008". Microsoft Corporation. 2008-04-28. Retrieved 2008-05-19.

[2] Romano, Benjamin J. (2008-04-29). "Microsoft device helps police pluck evidence from cyberscene of crime". The Seattle Times. Retrieved 2008-05-19.

[3] "Microsoft Calls on global public-private partnerships to Help in the Fight Against Cybercrime (Q&A with Tim Cranton, Associate General Counsel for Microsoft)". Microsoft Corporation. 2008-04-28. Retrieved 2008-05-19.

[4] "INTERPOL initiative with Microsoft aims to raise global standards against cybercrime through strategic partnership with IT sector". INTERPOL. Retrieved 2009-07-16.

[5] http://www.microsoft.com/industry/government/solutions/cofee/default.aspx

[6] "Microsoft COFEE law enforcement tool leaks all over the Internet". TechCrunch. Retrieved 2009-11-07.

[7] "More COFEE Please, on Second Thought". Retrieved 2009-11-09.

[8] Pullin, Alexandra. "Microsoft's not bothered about COFEE leak". The Inquirer. Retrieved 24 August 2010.

[9] Valich, Theo (2008-05-07). "Microsoft's new product goes against crime: Meet (Hot) COFEE". Tigervision Media. Retrieved 2008-05-19.

[10] Mills, Elinor (2008-04-29). "Microsoft hosts its own police academy". CNet News.com. Retrieved 2008-05-19.

[11] Michael, Bartolacci (2012). *Advancements and Innovations in Wireless Communications and Network Technologies*. IGI Global. p. 226. ISBN 1466621540. Retrieved 26 June 2015.

[12] Goodin, Dan (14 December 2009). "Hackers declare war on international forensics tool". The Register. Retrieved 15 December 2009.

[13] Eaton, Nick. "Anti-COFEE tool DECAF revealed as stunt". Seattle PI. Retrieved 26 June 2015.

[14] "DECAF Was Just a Stunt, Now Over". Slashdot. Retrieved 26 June 2015.

[15] "Anti-forensische tool DECAF geen hoax". Security.nl. Retrieved 26 June 2015.

[16] Zetter, Kim (14 December 2009). "Hackers Brew Self-Destruct Code to Counter Police Forensics". Wired.com. Retrieved 15 December 2009.

8.6 External links

- Official website

- "Microsoft Computer Online Forensic Evidence Extractor (COFEE)". Microsoft Corporation. Retrieved 2010-06-19.

- "Regular or Decaf? Tool launched to combat COFEE". Praetorian Prefect. Retrieved 2009-12-18.

- "Reactivating DECAF in Two Minutes". Praetorian Prefect. Retrieved 2009-12-18.

Chapter 9

The Coroner's Toolkit

The Coroner's Toolkit (or **TCT**) is a suite of free computer security programs by Dan Farmer and Wietse Venema designed to assist in digital forensic analysis. The suite runs under several Unix-related operating systems: FreeBSD, OpenBSD, BSD/OS, SunOS/Solaris, Linux, and HP-UX. TCT is released under the terms of the IBM Public License.

Parts of TCT can be used to aid analysis of and data recovery from other computer disasters.

TCT was superseded by The Sleuth Kit,[1] although TSK it is only partially based on TCT, it is accepted as the TCT official successor by TCT authors.[2]

9.1 References

[1] http://www.porcupine.org/forensics/tct.html

[2] http://www.porcupine.org/forensics/tct.html

9.2 External links

- Official home page
- Feature: The Coroner's Toolkit
- Frequently Asked Questions about The Coroner's Toolkit

Chapter 10

Cyber Insider Threat

Cyber Insider Threat, or CINDER, is a DARPA program to develop novel approaches to the detection of activities within military-interest networks that are consistent with the activities of cyber espionage, see.[1]

The CINDER threat is unlike other vulnerability based attacks in that the action taken by the initiator is not based on unauthorized access by unauthorized objects or authorized objects, it is based on the concept that authorized access by authorized objects will normally occur (along with their subsequent actions) within the security boundary. This object action will not be viewed as an attack, but normal use when analyzed by standard IDS-IPS, logging and expert systems. The CINDER Mission will be seen as an unauthorized disclosure once data exfiltration has been realized. At that time, the resultant CINDER Case would change all object actions related to the disclosure from "Authorized Use by an Authorized Object" to "Unauthorized Use by an Authorized Object".[2]

Note: For the initial CINDER case, the controlling agent".[3] will still be seen as an Authorized Object based on the fact that the security system has passed an evaluation for Assurance and Functionality.

The Cyber Insider Threat has continued to be a known issue since the mid-1980s. The following NIST material dated March 1994 - Internal Threats, shows how it was defined in its infancy.

"System controls are not well matched to the average organization's security policy. As a direct result, the typical user is permitted to circumvent that policy on a frequent basis. The administrator is unable to enforce the policy because of the weak access controls, and cannot detect the violation of policy because of weak audit mechanisms. Even if the audit mechanisms are in place, the daunting volume of data produced makes it unlikely that the administrator will detect policy violations. Ongoing research in integrity and intrusion detection promise to fill some of this gap. Until these research projects become available as products, systems will remain vulnerable to internal threats."[4]

10.1 CINDER Behaviors and Methods

10.1.1 CINDER Prerequisites

There are many prerequisite dimensions to CINDER activity, but one primary dimension must always be met. That is one of System Ownership. Prerequisite principles of system ownership and information dominance within the area of object action must be part of any CINDER mission.

10.1.2 CINDER System Ownership and Object Action

In CINDER action, each mission dimension and each resulting case issue can be distilled down to one entity, one agent.[3] and one action. At the specific time an agent completes an action, that entity, agent and action owns the environment they are transiting or using. And if they are successful in committing that specific transaction and are not interrupted or at least measured or monitored by the owner, that entity will have, if for only a moment in time, dominance and ownership over that object.[2]

10.2 CINDER Detection methods

10.2.1 Methods for Detecting Past CINDER Actions

To detect past CINDER activity when an exposure has been realized, one must reconcile all object actions (any exchange or transaction between two agents that can be measured or logged) and analyze the result.

24

10.2.2 Methods for Detecting Current and Future CINDER Actions

Present concepts of how one detects current or future CIN-DER activity has followed the same path as detecting past CINDER activity: A reconciliation of all data from all object action, then the application of heuristics, expert system logic and mining models to the data aggregated.[5] But building automated logic and analysis models have proved difficult since once again, the insider does not attack they use (authorized access by authorized objects). Breaking this "use" and "how they use" out in a system that has low assurance and a low percentage of reconciliation will always cause the system to produce far too many false positives for the method to be acceptable as a true CINDER security solution.

One main tenet of CINDER detection has become that only a system that has high assurance and high reconciliation can be controlled (Owned) to the extent that current and future CINDER actions can be identified, monitored or terminated.

10.3 Ongoing projects to detect CIN-DER action

10.3.1 Defense Advanced Research Projects Agency DARPA

DARPA has an ongoing **Cyber Insider Threat** or **CIN-DER** program to detect insider threats to computer systems. It is under DARPA's Strategic Technology Office (STO).[6][7] The project was timed to begin around 2010/2011.[8] In comparison with traditional computer security, CINDER assumes that malicious insiders already have access to the internal network; thus it attempts to detect a threat's "mission" through analysis of behavior rather than seeking to keep a threat out. The government documentation uses an analogy of the "tell" idea from the card game of poker.[6]

According to Ackerman in Wired, the impetus for the program came after Wikileaks disclosures such as the Afghan War documents leak. Robert Gates' philosophy of information in the military was to emphasize the access for frontline soldiers. In the face of mass-leaking, the CINDER type of response allows the military to continue that philosophy, rather than simply cutting off access to information en masse.[7] The project was started by Peiter Zatko, a former member of the L0pht and cDc who left DARPA in 2013.[9]

10.4 See also

- ECHELON, Thinthread, Trailblazer, Turbulence, PRISM (surveillance program) (NSA programs)

- Einstein (US-CERT program)

- Fusion center, Investigative Data Warehouse (FBI)

- PRODIGAL, ADAMS (DARPA)

10.5 References

[1] http://www.darpa.mil/Our_Work/I2O/Programs/Cyber-Insider_Threat_(CINDER).aspx

[2] "Mission and Case Analysis of Cyber Insider (CINDER) Methods within Military and Corporate Environments". CodeCenters International Training Press. Retrieved 2012-05-09.

[3] "Intelligent Agents: Theory and Practice" (PDF). Knowledge Engineering Review. Retrieved 2012-05-24.

[4] "Trends for the future - Internal Threats". NIST. Retrieved 2012-05-11.

[5] "DTIC Analysis and Detection of Malicious Insiders". DTIC Defense Technical Information Center - MITRE Corporation. Retrieved 2012-05-11.

[6] "Broad Agency Announcement Cyber Insider Threat (CINDER)". DARPA Strategic Technology Office. 2010-08-25. Retrieved 2011-12-06.

[7] Ackerman, Spencer (2010-08-31). "Darpa's Star Hacker Looks to WikiLeak-Proof Pentagon". *Wired*. Retrieved 2011-12-05.

[8] "DARPA seeks assistance with insider threats". infosecurity-magazine.com. 2010-08-30. Retrieved 2011-12-06.

[9] http://www.bloomberg.com/news/2013-04-15/google-s-motorola-mobility-taps-u-s-defense-agency-for-talent.html

Chapter 11

Cymmetria

Cymmetria, Inc. is a private American network security company that provides deception based cyber security solutions against advanced cyber threats, such as advanced persistent threats. the Company uses proprietary deception technology to detect and disable hackers and cyber threats.

11.1 Timeline

Cymmetria was founded in 2014. Major core investors include Felicis Ventures, Lumia Capital, Seedcamp and Y Combinator.[1] In 2015 the company took part in Y Combinator Accelerator program.[2]

11.2 See also

- Check Point
- Palo Alto Networks
- Cisco
- Fortinet
- Blue Coat Systems

11.3 References

[1] Natasha Lomas (27 Jun 2015). "YC-Backed Cymmetria Uses Virtual Machines To Decoy And Detect Hackers". *CrunchBase.*

[2] NY Combinator (29 Jun 2015). "Cymmetria (YC S15) Uses Virtual Machines To Decoy And Detect Hackers". *Y Combinator.*

11.4 External links

- Official website

- Cymmetria at TechCrunch.

Chapter 12

Detekt

Detekt is a free tool by Amnesty International, Digitale Gesellschaft, EFF, and Privacy International to scan for surveillance software on Microsoft Windows.[1]

It's intended for use by activists and journalists to scan for known spyware.

12.1 The tool

Detekt is available for free download.[2]

The tool doesn't guarantee detection of all spyware, nor is it meant to give a false sense of security, and should be used with other methods to combat malware and spyware.[1]

The Coalition Against Unlawful Surveillance Exports estimates that the global trade in surveillance technologies is worth more than 3 billion GBP annually.[3]

It's available in Amharic, Arabic, English, German, Italian, and Spanish.

12.2 Technical

The tool requires no installation, and is designed to scan for surveillance software on Windows PCs, from XP to Windows 8.1.[4]

The tool scans for current surveillance software, and after scanning, it will display a summary indicating if any spyware was found or not. It will generate a log file containing the details.

The tool doesn't guarantee absolute protection from surveillance software, as it scans for known spyware (at the time of release), which could be modified to circumvent detection, or new software would become available.[2] Therefore, a clean bill of health doesn't necessarily mean that the PC is free of surveillance software.

The website instructs the user to disconnect the internet connection, and close all applications, before running, and not to turn the connection back on if any spyware was found.

Detekt is released under the GPLv3 free license.[5]

Detekt was developed by Claudio Guarnieri with the help of Bill Marczack, Morgan Marquis-Boire, Eva Galperin, Tanya O'Carroll, Andre Meister, Jillian York, Michael Ligh, Endalkachew Chala.

Currently it's provided with patterns for the following malware: DarkComet RAT, XtremeRAT, BlackShades RAT, njRAT, FinFisher FinSpy, HackingTeam RCS, ShadowTech RAT, Gh0st RAT.[4]

12.3 See also

- Computer and network surveillance
- Computer surveillance in the workplace
- Internet censorship
- Internet privacy
- Freedom of information
- Tor (anonymity network)
- 2013 mass surveillance disclosures

12.4 References

[1] Lomas, Natasha (November 20, 2014). "Amnesty, EFF, Privacy International Put Out Free Anti-Surveillance Tool". TechCrunch. Retrieved November 20, 2014.

[2] "RESIST SURVEILLANCE". Retrieved November 20, 2014.

[3] Taylor, Matthew (November 20, 2014). "Amnesty backs Detekt tool to scan for state spyware on computers". The Guardian. Retrieved November 20, 2014.

[4] "botherder/detekt". Retrieved November 20, 2014.

[5] "LICENSE". November 20, 2014. Retrieved November 20, 2014.

12.5   External links

- Official website

- Latest release

Chapter 13

Device configuration overlay

Device configuration overlay (**DCO**) is a hidden area on many of today's hard disk drives (HDDs). Usually when information is stored in either the DCO or host protected area (HPA), it is not accessible by the BIOS, OS, or the user. However, certain tools can be used to modify the HPA or DCO. The system uses the IDENTIFY_DEVICE command to determine the supported features of a given hard drive, but the DCO can report to this command that supported features are nonexistent or that the drive is smaller than it actually is. To determine the actual size and features of a disk, the DEVICE_CONFIGURATION_IDENTIFY command is used, and the output of this command can be compared to the output of IDENTIFY_DEVICE to see if a DCO is present on a given hard drive. Most major tools will remove the DCO in order to fully image a hard drive, using the DEVICE_CONFIGURATION_RESET command. This permanently alters the disk, unlike with the host protected area (HPA), which can be temporarily removed for a power cycle.[1]

13.1 Uses

The Device Configuration Overlay (DCO), which was first introduced in the ATA-6 standard, "allows system vendors to purchase HDDs from different manufacturers with potentially different sizes, and then configure all HDDs to have the same number of sectors. An example of this would be using DCO to make an 80-gigabyte HDD appear as a 60-gigabyte HDD to both the (OS) and the BIOS.... Given the potential to place data in these hidden areas, this is an area of concern for computer forensics investigators. An additional issue for forensic investigators is imaging the HDD that has the HPA and or DCO on it. While certain vendors claim that their tools are able to both properly detect and image the HPA, they are either silent on the handling of the DCO or indicate that this is beyond the capabilities of their tool."[2]

13.2 How various forensics tools handle the DCO

13.2.1 Detection tools

Data Synergy's free ATATool utility can be used to detect an DCO from a Windows environment. The current version does not allow a DCO to be removed.[3]

13.2.2 Software imaging tools

Guidance Software's EnCase comes with a Linux-based tool that images hard drives called LinEn. LinEn 6.01 was validated by the National Institute of Justice (NIJ) in October 2008, and they found that "The tool does not remove either Host Protected Areas (HPAs) or DCOs. However, the Linux test environment automatically removed the HPA on the test drive, allowing the tool to image sectors hidden by an HPA. The tool did not acquire sectors hidden by a DCO."[4]

AccessData's FTK Imager 2.5.3.14 was validated by the National Institute of Justice (NIJ) in June 2008. Their findings indicated that "If a physical acquisition is made of a drive with hidden sectors in either a Host Protected Area or a Device Configuration Overlay, the tool does not remove either an HPA or a DCO. The tool did not acquire sectors hidden by an HPA."[5]

13.2.3 Hardware imaging tools

A variety of hardware imaging tools have been found to successfully detect and remove DCOs. The NIJ routinely tests digital forensics tools and these publications can be found at http://nij.ncjrs.gov/App/publications/Pub_search.aspx?searchtype=basic&category=99&location=top&PSID=55 or from NIST at http://www.nist.gov/itl/ssd/cs/cftt/cftt-disk-imaging.cfm

13.3   See also

- Host protected area (HPA)

- Master Boot Record (MBR)

- GUID Partition Table (GPT)

13.4   References

[1] Brian Carrier (2005). *File System Forensic Analysis.* Addison Wesley. p. 38.

[2] Mark K. Rogers; Mayank R. Gupta; Michael D. Hoeschele (September 2006). "Hidden Disk Areas: HPA and DCO" (PDF). Retrieved August 2010.

[3] Data Synergy UK (July 2015). "ATATool - Data Synergy Windows HPA/DCO Utility".

[4] National Institute of Justice (October 2008). "NIJ Test Results for Digital Data Acquisition Tool: EnCase LinEn 6.01" (PDF). p. 5. Retrieved September 2010.

[5] National Institute of Justice (June 2008). "NIJ Test Results for Digital Data Acquisition Tool: FTK Imager 2.5.3.14" (PDF). p. 6. Retrieved September 2010.

Chapter 14

DriveSavers

DriveSavers, Inc. is a computer hardware data recovery, digital forensics and eDiscovery firm located in Novato, California.[1][2] It was founded by CEO Jay Hagan and former company President Scott Gaidano in 1985.[3][4][5]

14.1 History

In 1985 former Jasmine Technologies executives Jay Hagan and Scott Gaidano founded DriveSavers, operating from Gaidano's condo with $1,400.[4][3][4][5][6] DriveSavers originally offered both hard drive repair and data recovery services, but the company dropped its drive repair services within its first eight months.[5] In 1992, DriveSavers signed an agreement with SuperMac Technology to assume technical support and warranty obligations for SuperMac Mass Storage Products.[7]

The company merged with Data Recovery Disk Repair in 1994 and retained the DriveSavers name.[4] In 2008, DriveSavers invested two million dollars to build a series of five ISO-certified cleanrooms, to diassemble and rebuild damaged hard drives.[8][1][4][6] From 2004-2009, the company grew from 35 to 85 employees.[9]

14.2 Services

DriveSavers is a "top-of-the-range" data recovery service. On average it can recover 90 percent of the files from a non-functioning storage device.[9] Recovering data from an iPhone can cost between $500 to $1,400.[10] It has a positive and well-respected reputation. 70 percent of its clients are corporations. It also works with "the more secretive" branches of government and celebrities.[3][9]

DriveSavers is the only recovery firm licensed with every major hard-drive manufacturer, so their work on a drive does not void the warranty.[3] It can recover data from hard disk drives, solid state drives, smart phones, servers, digital camera media and iOS devices.[8][2][11][12][13] DriveSavers

is certified HIPAA-compliant, undergoes annual SOC2 Type II reviews and has encryption training certificates from GuardianEdge, PGP, PointSec and Utimaco.[1][14]

14.3 Awards

Diamond Certified, 2013-14[15]

14.4 References

[1] Alex Wawro (June 5, 2013). "Smash smartphone. Throw it in the ocean. Hope DriveSavers doesn't get it.". PC World. Retrieved September 16, 2013.

[2] Mat Honan (August 17, 2012). "Mat Honan: How I Resurrected My Digital Life After an Epic Hacking". Wired. Retrieved September 16, 2013.

[3] Chris Taylor (June 3, 2003). "Fried Your Drive?". Time. Retrieved September 16, 2013.

[4] Tony C. Yang (August 31, 2008). "Saving the day by saving data". San Francisco Business Journal. Retrieved September 16, 2013.

[5] Christine Kilpatrick (April 9, 2000). "Cyber-saviors". San Francisco Business Journal. Retrieved September 16, 2013.

[6] Rik Myslewski (August 29, 2008). "Profile: DriveSavers stays true to data-recovery roots". MacWorld. Retrieved September 16, 2013.

[7] Mark H. Anbinder (September 14, 1992). "SuperMac & DriveSavers". TidBITS. Retrieved September 16, 2013.

[8] Neil J. Rubenking (March 10, 2010). "Inside the DriveSavers Clean Rooms". PC Magazine. Retrieved September 16, 2013.

[9] Chris Taylor (October 26, 2009). "The tech catastrophe you're ignoring". Fortune. Retrieved September 16, 2013.

[10] Suzanne Choney (July 15, 2009). "Smartphone 'whoops!' is painful and expensive". NBC News. Retrieved September 16, 2013.

[11] David Dahlquist (April 21, 2010). "DriveSavers Adds IPad Data Recovery Service". PCWorld. Retrieved September 16, 2013.

[12] Andy Ihnatko (September 19, 2012). "The camera from the bottom of the lagoon". TechHive. Retrieved September 16, 2013.

[13] Neil J. Rubenking (April 11, 2008). "What Drives Can DriveSavers Save?". PC Magazine. Retrieved September 16, 2013.

[14] "DriveSavers Answers Your Data Recovery Questions". FileSlinger. Retrieved September 16, 2013.

[15] http://www.diamondcertified.org/report/drivesavers-inc-0, retrieved December 19, 2014

14.5   External links

- Official site

Chapter 15

EnCase

"Encase" redirects here. For the coil, see encased coil. For the meaning of encase, see wikt:encase.

EnCase is the shared technology within a suite of digital investigations products by Guidance Software. The software comes in several products designed for forensic, cyber security, security analytics, and e-discovery use. The company also offers EnCase training and certification.

Data recovered by EnCase has been used in various court systems, such as in the cases of the BTK Killer and the murder of Danielle van Dam.[1][2]

15.1 EnCase Product Line

EnCase technology is available within a number of products, currently including: EnCase Forensic, EnCase Cybersecurity, EnCase eDiscovery, and EnCase Portable.[3] Guidance Software also runs training courses and certification, over 50,000 individuals have completed the training to date.[4]

15.2 Features

EnCase contains tools for several areas of the digital forensic process; acquisition, analysis and reporting. The software also includes a scripting facility called EnScript with various API's for interacting with evidence.

15.2.1 EnCase Evidence File Format

EnCase contains functionality to create forensic images of suspect media. Images are stored in proprietary *EnCase Evidence File Format*; the compressible file format is prefixed with case data information and consists of a bit-by-bit (i.e. exact) copy of the media inter-spaced with CRC hashes for every 64K of data. The file format also appends an MD5 hash of the entire drive as a footer.[5]

15.2.2 Mobile forensics

As of EnCase V7, Mobile Phone Analysis is possible with the addition some add-ons available from Guidance Software.[6]

15.3 References

[1] Taub, Eric A. (2006-04-05). "Deleting may be easy, but your hard drive still tells all". New York Times. Retrieved 2009-01-11.

[2] Dillon, Jeff, and Steve Perez. "Prosecutor hammers away at computer forensic expert; Dad's patron describes Brenda's propositions," San Diego Union-Tribune, July 3, 2002.

[3] url=http://www.guidancesoftware.com/"| 11 October 2012

[4] url="http://itbriefing.net/modules.php?op=modload&name=News&file=article&sid=328379" | 11 October 2012

[5] Martin S. Olivier, Sujeet Shenoi, ed. (2006). *Advances in digital forensics II*. Springer. ISBN 0-387-36890-6. Retrieved 31 August 2010.

[6] GuidanceSoftware. "EnCase Forensic V7". *GuidanceSoftware*. Retrieved 13 April 2012.

15.4 Further reading

- Garber, Lee. "EnCase: A Case Study in Computer-Forensic Technology" (PDF). IEEE Computer Society. Retrieved 10 November 2010.

15.5 External links

- Guidance Software web site

Chapter 16

FireEye

For the bird genus, see Fire-eye.

Warning: Page using Template:Infobox company with unknown parameter "market cap" (this message is shown only in preview).

FireEye, Inc. is a publicly listed US network security company that provides automated threat forensics and dynamic malware protection against advanced cyber threats, such as advanced persistent threats and spear phishing. Founded in 2004, the company is headquartered in Milpitas, California. Threat prevention platforms include Network, Email, Endpoint, Mobile, Content, Analytics, and Forensics. FireEye has more than 4,400 customers across 67 countries, including more than 650 of the Forbes Global 2000. FireEye is the first cyber security company awarded certification by the Department of Homeland Security.[1] USAToday says Fire-Eye "has been called in to investigate high-profile attacks against Target, JP Morgan Chase, Sony Pictures, Anthem and others".[2] Yahoo Finance says FireEye is again fastest growing cyber security firm, according to Deloitte.[3]

Dave DeWalt, CEO and Chairman of the Board of FireEye in South Korea, in June 2013

16.1   Foundation

In 2004, Ashar Aziz, a Pakistani American, founded Fire-Eye with venture capital provided by Sequoia Capital.[4] Aziz, formerly of Sun Microsystems, is the original inventor of the core set of technologies behind the company's main product line, the FireEye Malware Protection System.[5] In 2006, FireEye launched its first product—a switch-based network access control appliance.[6]

Major investors include Sequoia Capital, Norwest Venture Partners, Icon Ventures, SVB Capital,[7] DAG Ventures, Juniper Networks, and In-Q-Tel.[8]

16.2   Expansion

In June 2012, former CEO and President of McAfee, Dave DeWalt, joined FireEye as chairman.[9] DeWalt was appointed CEO in November 2012.[9][10]

On December 30, 2013, FireEye acquired Mandiant in a stock and cash deal worth in excess of $1 billion.[11]

On May 8, 2014, FireEye acquired company nPulse Technologies[12] for approximately $60 million. nPulse is intended to build on FireEye's ability to detect intrusions in a company's network by making it easier to track the intrusion and better understand its effect on the network.[13]

In May 2015, the company raised its revenue forecast for

the year to be between $615 million and $635 million.[14]

16.3 Products and services

16.3.1 Central Management System

The Central Management System (CMS) consolidates the management, reporting, and data sharing of Web MPS, Email MPS, File MPS, and Malware Analysis System (MAS) into a single network-based appliance by acting as a distribution hub for malware security intelligence.

16.3.2 Dynamic Threat Intelligence

The FireEye Cloud crowd-sources Dynamic Threat Intelligence (DTI) detected by individual FireEye MPS appliances, and automatically distributes this time sensitive zero-day intelligence globally to all subscribed customers in frequent updates. Content Updates include a combination of DTI and FireEye Labs generated intelligence identified through Research efforts.

16.4 Government

FireEye's solutions are available for the public sector through Carahsoft, their reseller network, and partners, through a large variety of contract vehicles including GSA Schedule 70, SEWP-V, CMaaS BPA, and various other state and local contracts.

16.5 Cyber actions

16.5.1 2008

FireEye was involved in the forensic investigation against the Srizbi botnet in 2008.[15][16]

16.5.2 2009

In October/November 2009, FireEye participated in an effort to take down the Mega-D botnet (also known as Ozdok.)[17]

16.5.3 2011

On March 16, 2011, the Rustock botnet was taken down through an action by Microsoft, US federal law enforcement

agents, FireEye, and the University of Washington.[18]

16.5.4 2012

In July 2012, FireEye was involved in analysis[19] of the Grum botnet's command and control servers located in the Netherlands, Panama, and Russia.

16.5.5 2015

In September 2015, FireEye obtained an injunction against a security researcher attempting to report vulnerabilities in FireEye Malware Protection System.[20]

16.6 See also

- Blue Coat Systems
- Check Point
- Cisco
- Fortinet
- Palo Alto Networks
- Zscaler

16.7 References

[1] "FireEye First Cyber Security Company Awarded SAFETY Act Certifications by Department of Homeland Security". *MarketWatch*. Retrieved 21 May 2015.

[2] "FireEye has become Go-to Company for Breaches". *USA Today*. Retrieved 21 May 2015.

[3] "FireEye Fastest Growing Cyber Security". *Yahoo Finance*. Retrieved 2015-11-20.

[4] Mitra, Sramana (January 29, 2009). "Barriers To Innovation". *Forbes*. Retrieved 2009-11-30.

[5] "Crunchbase — Ashar Aziz". Crunchbase. 2012-07-18. Retrieved 2012-07-18.

[6] Messmer, Ellen (2006-05-02). "Start-up FireEye debuts with virtual-machine security approach". *Network World*. Retrieved 2010-10-18.

[7] Jose Sevilla (3 August 2015). "Silicon Valley Bank - SVB Capital". *SVB Financial Group*.

[8] Hoover, J.Nicholas (November 19, 2009). "In-Q-Tel Joins Forces With FireEye To Fight Cyberthreats". DarkReading. Retrieved 2009-11-30.

[9] "FireEye Appoints Board Chairman David DeWalt as Chief Executive Officer" (Press release). FireEye. 2012-11-28. Retrieved 2012-11-30.

[10] Robertson, Jordan (2012-11-28). "Former McAfee Chief DeWalt Named FireEye CEO, Aims for 2013 IPO". Bloomberg. Retrieved 2012-11-30.

[11] Perlroth, Nicole; Sanger, David E. (2014-01-02). "FireEye Computer Security Firm Acquires Mandiant". *The New York Times*.

[12] "Computer Forensics and Malware Analysis - FireEye". *FireEye*.

[13] Miller, Ron (May 8, 2014). "FireEye Buys nPulse Technologies For $60M+ To Beef Up Network Security Suite". *TechCrunch*.

[14] Tony Owusu. "FireEye (FEYE) Stock Spikes on Earnings Beat, Increased Revenue Guidance". *TheStreet*. Retrieved August 4, 2015.

[15] Keizer, Gregg (November 26, 2008). "Massive botnet returns from the dead, starts spamming". *Computerworld*. Retrieved 2009-11-30.

[16] Kiriyama, George (November 11, 2008). "SJ-Based Spammer Unplugged". NBC 11 KNTV. Retrieved 2009-11-30.

[17] Cheng, Jacqui (November 11, 2009). "Researchers' well-aimed stone takes down Goliath botnet". Ars Technica. Retrieved 2009-11-30.

[18] Wingfield, Nick (2011-03-18). "Spam Network Shut Down". *Wall Street Journal*. Retrieved 2011-03-18.

[19] "FireEye Blog | Threat Research, Analysis, and Mitigation". Blog.fireeye.com. Retrieved 2014-04-12.

[20] Goodin, Dan (September 11, 2015). "Security company litigates to bar disclosure related to its own flaws". Retrieved September 12, 2015.

16.8 External links

- Official website

- FireEye: Botnet Busters - When Microsoft and Pfizer got fed up with the nastiest junk e-mail blaster on the Web, they called Silicon Valley's cybercrime vigilante June 16, 2011 Bloomberg BusinessWeek's Christopher S. Stewart

Chapter 17

Forensic corporate collections

Forensic Corporate Collections refer to the type of debt collection and recovery tactics that apply computer forensics and scientific knowledge to the debt collection process.

17.1 Process

By engaging consistently updated computer software in the debt collection process, forensic corporate collection agencies are able to identify, retrieve, and protect electronic evidence of fraud (and other illegal means of avoiding debt) found on computers and use it as evidence in case of litigation. In order for a forensic collections agency to be used as a means of recovering a debt, the agency must be compliant with and knowledgeable of investigation basics, federal, state and local policies, standards, laws and legal processes. They must also have a working knowledge of the types of crimes and incidents in debt deception and fraud, the computing environment and types of evidence, as well as investigative tools, technical training, and use of forensic recovery equipment.

In order to effectively recover and locate debtors and get them to pay what they owe their client(s), forensic collections agents have become adept and conversant in evidence collection and management, managing the incident scene, the investigation of computer systems, disks, and file structures, extracting and preserving computer and electronic evidence, e-mail and Internet investigations, cell phone and PDA investigations, and other digital footprints debtors invariably leave behind.

Chapter 18

Forensic search

Forensic Search is an emerging field of computer forensics. Forensic Search focuses on user created data such as email files, cell phone records, office documents, PDFs and other files that are easily interpreted by a person.

Forensic Search differs from computer forensic analysis in that it does not seek to review or analyze the lower level system files such as the registry, link files or disk level issues more commonly associated with traditional computer forensic analysis.

18.1 Why Forensic Search

Forensic Search has emerged due to a number of factors including:

- Improvements in technologies to enable lesser qualified users to undertake search and analysis of data that would have previously been undertaken only by a computer forensic expert. (This trend can be seen in many industries).

- A need to reduce the high cost of undertaking a full computer forensic analysis of a user's computer, when in most cases the evidence found in the user created data is most useful and all that is required.

- The rise of Cloud computing which has seen a move away from data storage on local computer hardware to data storage in any number of remote locations.[1]

- A lack of qualified computer forensic experts

- The need to address the backlog of cases in most policing agencies where computer-based information requires review.[2][3]

- The need to involve other types of expertise for proper assessment of evidence, e.g. knowledge of accounting regulations, legal knowledge, etc.

18.2 Forensic Search Objectives

The objective of Forensic Search software is to allow a person with only a general knowledge of computers, but skilled in document review or investigation techniques, to undertake and search user created Electronically Stored Information (ESI). Data that is typically considered to be user created ESI is made up of emails, documents, pictures and other file types created by a user, as opposed to data created by the computer's operating system (i.e. registry files, link files, unallocated space. These are controlled or created by the computer and not the user). The objective of reviewing the user created data is to find information that may be used to base decisions on as part of an investigation.

18.3 Advantages of Forensic Search Software

Forensic Search software differs from using the native applications (e.g. Outlook) or desktop search software (e.g. Google desktop) to search the data in that no changes are made to the data during processing or searching that may impact the results or skew the findings. Forensic Search software will also allow access to the base metadata of items not available via the native application. A good example of this would be the metadata in MS Word documents.[4] A number of Forensic Search software products will be able to perform data recovery on a range of email file types.

Some examples of how using the native application or non-forensic application can affect the data:

- Opening a Microsoft Word document in Microsoft Word may change the created, modified or last accessed dates in the document. This could lead to the incorrect dates being supplied in evidence.

- Reviewing data in some native applications will trigger the systems Antivirus, again changing data or altering evidence.

- Failure to freeze the evidence prior to opening the files, coupled with the fact that merely opening the files changes them, can and has invalidated critical evidence.[5]

18.4 Other Types of Review

Forensic Search software has been likened to eDiscovery review software, however this is not strictly the case. eDiscovery review software, while dealing with many of the same type of computer records and search options, offer extra functionality to that of Forensic Search software. Features such as redaction and legal hold are standard in eDiscovery review software. It is also the case that Forensic Search software does not meet with the higher end tasks outlined in the widely accepted Electronic Discovery Reference Model (EDRM). Tasks such as Identification, Collection, Preservation or Presentation are generally not covered by Forensic Search software.

However, true eDiscovery review is generally the domain of qualified legal practitioners or companies.[6][7]

The use of the term eDiscovery has become a catchall in some circles for the processing and searching of Electronically Stored Information (ESI). However, this is not a true representation of the term of eDiscovery. For a more detailed understanding of eDiscovery, the Electronic Discovery Reference Model (EDRM) is a good guideline.

It could be said that Forensic Search is more closely related to Early Case Assessment (ECA) than eDiscovery as ECA does not require the rigor of a full eDiscovery review.

18.5 Evidence Values of User Created Data Versus Other Types of Data

When presenting data as part of a report that may be used to form a decision or as evidence, it is important that the data be correctly represented so the reader can understand it.

In the case of generating reports on system created data such as registry files, link files and other system created data this can be a costly exercise. It can also be the case that there is no straightforward answer or explanation.

An example of this would be attempting to explain to a lay person the method and techniques of decoding the UserAssist Key in the Windows System Registry. The UserAssist key can hold a great deal of information about the actions of the user of the computer. However to explain this key, the reviewer has to be able to identify the key and correctly interpret the key setting. The keys are often encoded by ROT 13.

Once these keys are decoded to human readable formats, the reviewer then has to show how a setting relates to the case. It is often time consuming to review hundreds, even thousands, of settings that at times only deliver very circumstantial and sometimes contentious findings.

When reviewing user created data such as e-mail or contracts, reporting and understanding the findings is often much more straight forward. The semi skilled user will usually have a good grasp of how email works as they use it in their day-to-day work. A legal person will understand a contract and does not need specialist forensic knowledge to do so. This can lead to much lower costs of review and less contentious or circumstantial findings.

18.6 High-Level Functionality of Forensic Search Software

The features of Forensic Search software are focused on allowing the user to search and view a range of data and users' files at one time.

Specific features of Forensic Search software are:

- The ability to process varying types of data enabling it to be searched by the reviewer with little or no computer forensic knowledge

- Keyword searching across all data and data types processed

- The ability to create complex searches such as including or excluding data

- Using MD5 and other algorithms to search and identify files and data

- The ability to filter based on metadata such as dates, email addresses and file types

- The ability to review different data typed in the same search results

- The ability to view all results in the same user interface

- The ability to export items to various formats i.e. email, Word, HTML

- The ability to create shareable reports

18.7   Changes in Computer Forensics

There are many newer and emerging fields of computer forensics such as Cloud forensics, Mobile Phone forensics, Network forensics, Memory Analysis, Browser forensics, forensic triage and Internet forensics.[8] In the not so distant past a computer forensic expert's most common role was to attend a person's house, place of work or data center to forensically 'image' all computers or devices that may be involved in a case. This was categorized as the collection phase.

Once collection phase was complete these images were reviewed and the ESI that was relevant was supplied to the interested parties. This required the computer forensic investigator to have a good deal of experience and training in:

- Identifying which computer, applications or devices may be involved

- How to disassemble a computer and extract the hard drives of the computer without causing damage.

- How to correctly take a forensic image to keep chain of custody

- How to use the forensic analysis software to correctly interpret and supply the results

This process was time consuming and costly. The computer forensic expert's primary role is to investigate the computer evidence (ESI). They may not have been as familiar with the entire case or objectives as that of the case agent, detective, forensic accountant or crime analyst. This often led to non-perfect or time consuming identification of the correct evidence items between the differing parties. What would immediately flag the interest of a detective with a deep knowledge of the case and parties involved may go unnoticed by a computer forensic expert. An example would be an email from a suspect in another case to a suspect in this case, or contact / phone calls to a witness from a suspect.

To compound the issue, there has been a massive increase in the size of the data that the computer forensic expert needs to collect. It is now often the case that the computer hard drive is not able to be imaged, for example if the computer that contains the evidence is too big, or the system cannot be shut down to take an image as it is a mission critical server such as an email server or company file server. The rise of Cloud computing has also added challenges to the collection of evidence. The data that requires collection and review may reside in the Cloud. In this case there is no computer available to image. The forensic expert then needs to collect the information using forensic software designed to work with certain Cloud providers.[9]

In short the collection of evidence has changed significantly in the past few years.

18.8   Barriers to the Adoption of Forensic Search in Law Enforcement

Law enforcement organizations like many other organizations are divided into skill specific units. In the computer forensic / cybercrime area these units take responsibility for all aspects of the ESI. As discussed in "Why Forensic Search" point 5 these units are usually time poor and under resourced.

Albeit that time and resources are low the main knowledge in the unit comes from officers or consultants with 7+ years of experience (this predates most computer forensic degrees available). These officers have become familiar over time with the methodology of using a Forensic Analysis software package as this is all that was on offer when they started in the field. Hence when new officers or resources become available it is forensic analysis software that is prioritized over newer more specific software and newer forensic field types.

18.9   Conclusion

Forensic Search software has become popular as a method of reducing the time and cost of search and analysis of larger data sets by focusing on the user data that most often yields evidence or results.

E-mail is such seductive, powerful evidence. It's personal, plentiful and candid. For most adults, e-mail is their primary means of written communication. When lawyers think "e-discovery," it's the e-mail they crave. No surprise, then, that e-mail traffic is the most sought-after and fought-over ESI.[10]

18.10   References

[1] Crawford, Stephanie (2011-08-08). "HowStuffWorks "Are my files really safe if I store them in the cloud?"". Computer.howstuffworks.com. Retrieved 2012-10-24.

[2] "Backlog at Maine Computer Crimes Unit keeps child pornographers on the streets — State — Bangor Daily News — BDN Maine". Bangordailynews.com. 2011-11-25. Retrieved 2012-10-24.

[3] Matrix Group International, Inc. Alexandria, VA 2003 http: //www.matrixgroup.net. "View Article". Police Chief Magazine. Retrieved 2012-10-24.

[4] "Microsoft Word bytes Tony Blair in the butt". Computerbytesman.com. Retrieved 2012-10-24.

[5] http://euro.ecom.cmu.edu/program/law/08-732/Evidence/ RyanShpantzer.pdf

[6] "Ethics Opinion 362: Non-lawyer Ownership of Discovery Service Vendors". Dcbar.org. 2012-01-12. Retrieved 2012-10-24.

[7] "District of Columbia Bar: eDiscovery Vendors with Non-Lawyers Can't Practice Law". IT-Lex. 2012-07-11. Retrieved 2012-10-24.

[8]

[9] "F-Response 4.0.4 and the new Cloud Connector". F-response.com. 2012-07-24. Retrieved 2012-10-24.

[10] http://www.craigball.com/BIYC.pdf

Chapter 19

Forensic Toolkit

Forensic Toolkit, or FTK, is a computer forensics software made by AccessData. It scans a hard drive looking for various information.[1] It can for example locate deleted emails[2] and scan a disk for text strings to use them as a password dictionary to crack encryption.[3]

The toolkit also includes a standalone disk imaging program called **FTK Imager**. The FTK Imager is a simple but concise tool. It saves an image of a hard disk in one file or in segments that may be later on reconstructed. It calculates MD5 hash values and confirms the integrity of the data before closing the files. The result is an image file(s) that can be saved in several formats including, DD raw.

19.1 References

[1] Schneier, Bruce (2007-11-01). "Secure Passwords Keep You Safer". Wired. p. 3. Retrieved 2009-01-12.

[2] Dixon, Phillip D. (December 2005). "An overview of computer forensics" (PDF). *IEEE Potentials* (IEEE) **24** (5): 8. doi:10.1109/mp.2005.1594001. ISSN 0278-6648. Retrieved 2009-01-12.

[3] Casey, Eoghan (Fall 2002). "Practical Approaches to Recovering Encrypted Digital Evidence" (PDF). *International Journal of Digital Evidence* (Utica, New York: Economic Crime Institute, Utica College) **1** (3): 12. ISSN 1938-0917. Retrieved 2009-01-12.

19.2 External links

AccessData Forensic Toolkit Version 5.5

Chapter 20

HashKeeper

HashKeeper is a database application of value primarily to those conducting forensic examinations of computers on a somewhat regular basis.

20.1 Overview

HashKeeper uses the MD5 file signature algorithm to establish unique numeric identifiers (hash values) for files "known to be good" and "known to be bad."

The HashKeeper application was developed to reduce the amount of time required to examine files on digital media. Once an examiner defines a file as known to be good, the examiner need not repeat that analysis.

HashKeeper compares hash values of known to be good files against the hash values of files on a computer system. Where those values match "known to be good" files, the examiner can say, with substantial certainty, that the corresponding files on the computer system have been previously identified as known to be good and therefore do not need to be examined.

Where those values match known to be bad files, the examiner can say with substantial certainty that the corresponding files on the system being examined that the files are bad and therefore require further scrutiny. A hash match on known to be bad files does not relieve the examiner of the responsibility of verifying that the file or files are, in fact, of a criminal nature.

20.2 History

Created by the National Drug Intelligence Center (NDIC)—a component of the United States Department of Justice—in 1996, it was the first large scale source for hash values of "known to be good" and "known to be bad" files. HashKeeper was, and still is, the only community effort based upon the belief that members of state, national, and international law enforcement agencies can be trusted to submit properly categorized hash values. One of the first community sources of "known to be good" hash values was the United States Internal Revenue Service. The first source of "known to be bad" hash values was the Luxembourg Police who contributed hash values of recognized child pornography.

20.3 Availability

HashKeeper is available, free-of-charge, to law enforcement, military and other government agencies throughout the world. It is available to the public by sending a Freedom of Information Act request to NDIC.

In the 2012 United States budget, NDIC was de-funded and closed its doors on June 16, 2012. The availability and future of HashKeeper is uncertain.

20.4 Source

HashKeeper Overview, National Drug Intelligence Center.

20.5 See also

- National Software Reference Library
- Rainbow table

20.6 References

http://www.justice.gov/archive/ndic/ndic-moved.html

http://www.nsrl.nist.gov/nsrl-faqs.html#faq12

Chapter 21

Host protected area

"BEER" redirects here. For other uses, see Beer (disambiguation).

The **host protected area** (also referred to as **hidden protected area**[1]) is an area of a hard drive that is not normally visible to an operating system (OS).

21.1 History

HPA was first introduced in the ATA-4 standard cxv (T13, 2001).[2]

21.2 How it works

The IDE controller has registers that contain data that can be queried using ATA commands. The data returned gives information about the drive attached to the controller. There are three ATA commands involved in creating and using a hidden protected area. The commands are:

- IDENTIFY DEVICE
- SET MAX ADDRESS
- READ NATIVE MAX ADDRESS

Operating systems use the IDENTIFY DEVICE command to find out the addressable space of a hard drive. The IDENTIFY DEVICE command queries a particular register on the IDE controller to establish the size of a drive.

This register however can be changed using the SET MAX ADDRESS ATA command. If the value in the register is set to less than the actual hard drive size then effectively a host protected area is created. It is protected because the OS will work with only the value in the register that is returned by the IDENTIFY DEVICE command and thus will normally be unable to address the parts of the drive that lie within the HPA.

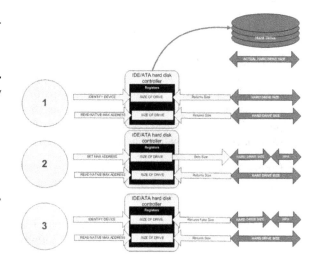

Creation of an HPA. The diagram shows how a host protected area (HPA) is created.
1. IDENTIFY DEVICE returns the true size of the hard drive. READ NATIVE MAX ADDRESS returns the true size of the hard drive.
2. SET MAX ADDRESS reduces the reported size of the hard drive. READ NATIVE MAX ADDRESS returns the true size of the hard drive. An HPA has been created.
3. IDENTIFY DEVICE returns the now fake size of the hard drive. READ NATIVE MAX ADDRESS returns the true size of the hard drive, the HPA is in existence.

The HPA is useful only if other software or firmware (e.g. BIOS) is able to use it. Software and firmware that are able to use the HPA are referred to as 'HPA aware'. The ATA command that these entities use is called READ NATIVE MAX ADDRESS. This command accesses a register that contains the true size of the hard drive. To use the area, the controlling HPA-aware program changes the value of the register read by IDENTIFY DEVICE to that found in the register read by READ NATIVE MAX ADDRESS. When its operations are complete, the register read by IDENTIFY DEVICE is returned to its original fake value.

21.3 Use

- At the time HPA was first implemented on Hard Disk firmware, some BIOS had difficulty booting with large Hard Disks. An initial HPA could then be set (by some jumpers on the Hard Disk) to limit the number of cylinder to 4095 or 4096 so that older BIOS would start. It was then the job of the bootloader to reset the HPA so that the operating system would see the full Hard Disk storage space.

- HPA can be used by various booting and diagnostic utilities, normally in conjunction with the BIOS. An example of this implementation is the Phoenix FirstBIOS, which uses **BEER** (Boot Engineering Extension Record) and **PARTIES** (Protected Area Run Time Interface Extension Services).[3] Another example is the Gujin installer which can install the bootloader in **BEER**, naming that pseudo-partition /dev/hda0 or /dev/sdb0; then only cold boots (from power-down) will succeed because warm boots (from Control-Alt-Delete) will not be able to read the HPA.

- Computer manufacturers may use the area to contain a preloaded OS for install and recovery purposes (instead of providing DVD or CD media).

- Dell notebooks hide Dell MediaDirect utility in HPA. IBM and LG notebooks hide system restore software in HPA.

- HPA is also used by various theft recovery and monitoring service vendors. For example, the laptop security firm Computrace use the HPA to load software that reports to their servers whenever the machine is booted on a network. HPA is useful to them because even when a stolen laptop has its hard drive formatted the HPA remains untouched.

- HPA can also be used to store data that is deemed illegal and is thus of interest to government and police computer forensics teams.[4]

- Some vendor-specific external drive enclosures (Maxtor) are known to use HPA to limit the capacity of unknown replacement hard drives installed into the enclosure. When this occurs, the drive may appear to be limited in size (e.g. 128 GB), which can look like a BIOS or dynamic drive overlay (DDO) problem. In this case, one must use software utilities (see below) that use READ NATIVE MAX ADDRESS and SET MAX ADDRESS to change the drive's reported size back to its native size, and avoid using the external enclosure again with the affected drive.

- Some rootkits hide in the HPA to avoid being detected by anti-rootkit and antivirus software.[3]

- Some NSA exploits use the HPA[5] for application persistence.

21.4 Identification and manipulation

Identification of HPA on a hard drive can be achieved by a number of tools and methods.

Note that the HPA feature can be hidden by DCO commands (documentation states only if the HPA is not in use), and can be "frozen" (until next power-down of the hard disk) or be password protected.

21.4.1 Identification tools

- The Sleuth Kit (free, open software) by Brian Carrier. (HPA identification is currently Linux-only.)

- ATATool, by Data Synegy is a free Windows-based HPA tool

- The ATA Forensics Tool (TAFT)[6] by Arne Vidstrom.

- EnCase by Guidance Software

- Access Data's Forensic Toolkit

- X-Ways Forensics, by X-Ways Software Technology AG

21.4.2 Identification methods

Using Linux, there are various ways to detect the existence of an HPA. Recent versions of Linux will print a message when the system is booting if an HPA is detected. For example:

dmesg | less [...] hdb: Host Protected Area detected. current capacity is 12000 sectors (6 MB) native capacity is 120103200 sectors (61492 MB)

The program hdparm (versions 8.0 and above) will detect an HPA on drive sdX when invoked with these parameters:

hdparm -N /dev/sdX

For versions of hdparm below 8, one can compare the number of sectors output from 'hdparm -I' with the number of sectors reported for the hard drive model's published statistics.

21.4.3   Manipulation tools

Creating and manipulating HPA on a hard drive can be achieved by a number of tools.

- HPARemove[7] by Aron Molnar.

- ATATool, by Data Synegy is a Windows-based HPA tool

- HDAT2[8] by Lubomir Cabla.

- setmax[9] by Andries E. Brouwer

- Feature Tool[10] by Hitachi Global Storage Technologies.

- MHDD (created by Dmitry Postrigan) is a freeware tool for hard drives that among other low-level functionalities provides information about the HPA state of a disk and can manipulate it.

- hdparm is a Linux program for reading and writing ATA and SATA hard drive parameters.

- FreeBSD has the hw.ata.setmax sysctl which can be set to 1.

- The Gujin bootloader [11] will remove the HPA if some disk partition cross the HPA limit, and freeze HPA & DCO before running the operating system.

21.4.4   Manipulation methods

The Linux program hdparm (version >= 8.0) will create an HPA when invoked with these parameters: (sdX: target drive, #: number of non-HPA visible sectors)

hdparm -N p# /dev/sdX

21.5   See also

- Device Configuration Overlay (DCO)

- Master Boot Record (MBR)

- GUID Partition Table (GPT)

21.6   References

[1] Hidden Protected Area - ThinkWiki

[2] Host Protected Areas

[3] Blunden, Bill. The Rootkit Arsenal: Escape and Evasion in the Dark Corners of the System. 1st ed. Jones & Bartlett Publishers, 2009 p.538

[4] Nelson, Bill; Phillips, Amelia; Steuart, Christopher (2010). *Guide to computer forensics and investigations* (4th ed.). Boston: Course Technology, Cengage Learning. p. 334. ISBN 1-435-49883-6.

[5] https://www.schneier.com/blog/archives/2014/02/swap_nsa_exploi.html

[6] vidstrom.net - security tools

[7] https://blog.itsecure.at/hparemove/

[8] HDAT2/CBL Hard Disk Repair Utility

[9] http://www.win.tue.nl/~{}aeb/linux/setmax.c

[10] Support - Downloads and Utilities

[11] http://sourceforge.net/projects/gujin/

21.7   External links

- The Sleuth Kit

- International Journal of Digital Evidence

- Dublin City University Security & Forensics wiki

- Wiki Web For ThinkPad Users

Chapter 22

Lastline

Lastline, Inc. is an American cyber security company and breach detection platform provider based in Redwood City, California.[1][2] The company offers network-based security breach detection and other security services that combat malware used by advanced persistent threat (APT) groups for businesses, government organizations and other security service providers.[3] Lastline has offices in North America, Europe, and Asia.[4]

22.1 History

Lastline was founded in 2011 by University of California, Santa Barbara and Northeastern University researchers Engin Kirda, Christopher Kruegel and Giovanni Vigna.[5] In 2014, WatchGuard Technologies, Inc. joined the Lastline Defense Program to combat advanced malware targeting businesses by providing primary functionality for APT blocking, available on their unified threat management (UTM) and next generation firewall (NGFW) products.[6] WatchGuard utilizes Lastline's next generation cloud-based sandbox, powered by full-system emulation, which inspects objects for unknown malware crafted to evade detection.[7]

Lastline was featured at the 2014 RSA Conference in San Francisco.[8] That same year, Giovanni Vigna, CTO at Lastline, appeared at the Cyber Security Expo in a keynote presentation that analyzed evasive malware techniques.[9]

Juniper Networks began integrating with Lastline to expand the capability of its Spotlight Secure platform in

2014.[10][11] In February 2015, Lastline announced a partnership and technology integration with Bit9 + Carbon Black in an effort to facilitate automated and comprehensive end-to-end endpoint and network security for email, web, files and mobile applications.[12][13]

22.2 Funding

In 2013, Lastline raised $10 million in funding led by venture capital firms Redpoint Ventures and E.ventures.[14] Redpoint Ventures led the Series B round with a $9 million investment, while existing investor E.ventures provided the remainder. [15] Regarding this funding, Jens Andreassen, CEO of Lastline said "This...will further propel our business to new levels as we continue to focus on our products in the channel and continue our research to develop even more solutions to help organizations protect their networks from rapidly evolving threats."[5]

In 2014, Lastline raised $10 million from new investors Dell Ventures and Presidio Ventures, as well as existing investors Redpoint Ventures and e.ventures.[16] With the new round of funding, Lastline will continue to focus on serving its growing global enterprise customer base as well as new and existing partnerships to improve information security and threat intelligence worldwide.[17] This round of funding adds to the $13.7 million raised in earlier rounds to bring total funding raised to nearly $24 million since the company's founding in 2011.[18]

22.3 Offerings

- Lastline Breach Detection Platform provides businesses with automated detection of active data breaches.

- Lastline Knowledge Base (LLKB) allows for access of information regarding historical data breach events, related IP addresses, and indicators of compromise

(IOCs) for malware linked to an advanced threat incident.

22.4 Lastline Labs

From May 2013 to May 2014 Lastline researchers studied hundreds of thousands of malware samples, testing new malware against 47 vendors' AV signatures featured in VirusTotal to determine which caught the malware samples, and how quickly.[19] They found that, on any given day, at least half of the AV scanners it tested failed to detect new malware and after two months, a third of the scanners were still not detecting it.[20][21]

22.5 See also

- Computer security

- Countermeasure (computer)

- IT risk

- Threat (computer)

22.6 References

[1] Yokwicz, Will Watching the (Digital) Detectives Rout Out Cyber Fraudsters *Inc.* March 4, 2015

[2] Goldman, Jeff Data Breach Roundup: January 2014 *eSecurity Planet.* March 4, 2015

[3] Simonelli, Luca The Lastline of APT defence *IT Security Guru.* March 4, 2015

[4] Blue Coat Launches Encrypted Traffic Management Ready Certification Program *CNN Money.* March 5, 2015

[5] Lennon, Mike Lastline Raises $10 Million to Help Combat Targeted Attacks *SecurityWeek.* March 4, 2015

[6] Ohlhorst, Frank WatchGuard Brings Advanced Persistent Threat Protection (APT) to the Masses *Enterprise Networking Planet.* March 4, 2015

[7] Lastline Announces WatchGuard Technologies Joins Company's Defense Program to Deliver APT Protection Capabilities *Business Wire.* March 4, 2015

[8] Solomon, Howard RSA Conference roundup: Fortinet, HP announce security products *IT World Canada.* March 4, 2015

[9] Fisher, Paul Chasing and detecting evasive malware *IT Pro Portal.* March 4, 2015

[10] Bradley, Tony Juniper expands threat intelligence for more effective network defense *CSO.* March 4, 2015

[11] Kerner, Sean Michael Juniper Brings Increased Security Intelligence to SRX Gateway *Enterprise Networking Planet.* March 5, 2015

[12] Lastline Partners with Bit9 + Carbon Black to Deliver Comprehensive Network and Endpoint Breach Protection *Yahoo! Finance.* March 4, 2015

[13] Westervelt, Robert Growing List Of Security Partners Trigger Bit9 Carbon Black Growth *CRN.* March 5, 2015

[14] Lastline Obtains $10,000,000 New Financing Round *Xconomy.* March 4, 2015

[15] Denne, Scott Lastline Secures $10M for Behavior-Based Cybersecurity *Dow Jones.* March 4, 2015

[16] The Daily Startup: Jaunt Raises $27.8 Million For Virtual Reality Tech *Wall Street Journal.* March 4, 2015

[17] Drake, Sarah Malware detector Lastline raises $10M from Dell, Presidio *Silicon Valley Business Journal.* March 4, 2015

[18] Lastline Secures $10 Million Funding Round *Venture Beat.* March 4, 2015

[19] Engin, Kirda Most Antivirus Software Is Lousy At Detecting Advanced Malware *Forbes.* March 4, 2015

[20] Robinson, Brian Is antivirus now useless? *GCN.* March 4, 2015

[21] Dunn, John E. Antivirus software can't keep up with new malware, Lastline Labs analysis finds *tech world.* March 4, 2015

22.7 External links

- Official website

Chapter 23

MAC times

MAC times are pieces of file system metadata which record when certain events pertaining to a computer file occurred most recently. The events are usually described as "modification" (the data in the file was modified), "access" (some part of the file was read), and "metadata change" (the file's permissions or ownership were modified), although the acronym is derived from the "mtime", "atime", and "ctime" structures maintained by Unix file systems. Windows file systems do not update ctime when a file's metadata is changed, instead using the field to record the time when a file was first created, known as "creation time" or "birth time". Some other systems also record birth times for files, but there is no standard name for this metadata; ZFS, for example, stores birth time in a field called "crtime". MAC times are commonly used in computer forensics.[1][2] The name Mactime was originally coined by Dan Farmer, who wrote a tool with the same name.[3]

23.1 Modification time (mtime)

A file's modification time describes when the content of the file most recently changed. Because most file systems do not compare data written to a file with what is already there, if a program overwrites part of a file with the same data as previously existed in that location, the modification time will be updated even though the contents did not technically change.

23.2 Access time (atime)

A file's access time identifies when the file was most recently opened for reading. Access times are usually updated even if only a small portion of a large file is examined. A running program can maintain a file as "open" for some time, so the time at which a file was opened may differ from the time data was most recently read from the file.

Because some computer configurations are much faster at reading data than at writing it, updating access times after every read operation can be very expensive. Some systems mitigate this cost by storing access times at a coarser granularity than other times; by rounding access times only to the nearest hour or day, a file which is read repeatedly in a short time frame will only need its access time updated once.[4] In Windows, this is addressed by waiting for up to an hour to flush updated access dates to the disk.[5]

Some systems also provide options to disable access time updating altogether. In Windows, starting with Vista, file access time updating is disabled by default.[6]

23.3 Change time and creation time (ctime)

Unix and Windows file systems interpret 'ctime' differently:

- **Unix systems** maintain the historical interpretation of ctime as being the time when certain file metadata, *not its contents*, were last changed, such as the file's permissions or owner (e.g. 'This file's metadata was *changed* on 05/05/02 12:15pm').

- **Windows systems** use ctime to mean 'creation time' (also called 'birth time') (e.g. 'This file was *created* on 05/05/02 12:15pm').

This difference in usage can lead to incorrect presentation of time metadata when a file created on a Windows system is accessed on a Unix system and vice versa. Most Unix file systems don't store the creation time, although some, such as HFS+, ZFS, and UFS2 do. NTFS stores both the creation time and the change time.

The semantics of creation times is the source of some controversy. One view is that creation times should refer to the actual content of a file: e.g. for a digital photo the creation time would note when the photo was taken or first stored on a computer. A different approach is for creation times to stand for when the file system object itself was created,

49

e.g. when the photo file was last restored from a backup or moved from one disk to another.

23.4 Metadata issues

As with all file system metadata, user expectations about MAC times can be violated by programs which are not metadata-aware. Some file-copying utilities will explicitly set MAC times of the new copy to match those of the original file, while programs that simply create a new file, read the contents of the original, and write that data into the new copy, will produce new files whose times do not match those of the original.

Some programs, in an attempt to avoid losing data if a write operation is interrupted, avoid modifying existing files. Instead, the updated data is written to a new file, and the new file is moved to overwrite the original. This practice loses the original file metadata unless the program explicitly copies the metadata from the original file. Windows is not affected by this due to a workaround feature called **File System Tunneling**.[7]

23.5 See also

- Computer forensics

23.6 References

[1] Luque, Mark E. (2002). "Logical Level Analyses of Linux Systems". In Casey, E. *Handbook of Computer Crime Investigation: Forensic Tools and Technology*. London: Academic Press. pp. 182–183. ISBN 0-12-163103-6.

[2] Sheldon (2002). "Forensic Analyses of Windows Systems". In Casey, E. *Handbook of Computer Crime Investigation: Forensic Tools and Technology*. London: Academic Press. pp. 134–135. ISBN 0-12-163103-6.

[3] Dan Farmer (October 1, 2000). "What Are MACtimes?". Dr Dobb's Journal.

[4] "File Times". Microsoft MSDN Library.

[5] "File Times". Microsoft MSDN Library.

[6] "Disabling Last Access Time in Windows Vista to improve NTFS performance". The Storage Team at Microsoft.

[7] "Windows NT Contains File System Tunneling Capabilities". Microsoft Support.

23.7 External links

- Discussion about Windows and Unix timestamps (Cygwin project mailing list)

Chapter 24

MailXaminer

MailXaminer[1] is a digital forensic program[2][3][4] built to allow the examination of email messages from both web & application based email clients. The application is being developed by SysTools Software, with the slogan 'Simplifying Email Forensics'.[5] MailXaminer first loads messages from the chosen email storage source and arranges them hierarchically for the purpose of evidence analysis and extraction. The product name derived from a combination of 'Mail' and 'Examiner', denoting it as a platform to examine emails. The programming of the application provides carving out of deleted evidence or evidence from damaged sources in cases of evidence spoliation.[6] Post analysis, the software[7] serves output generation in court admissible digital formats (e.g. Concordance, Adobe PDF).

24.1 Overview

SysTools is the official developer of MailXaminer that launched its first release on December 1st, 2013. Subsequent allotment of official product licensing for constant screening of MailXaminer was given to SysTools Software Pvt. Ltd. At present, the most stable release of the product is version 4.6 and was launched in the year 2014[8] with added capabilities serving skin tone analysis, link analysis, and more.[9] The program helped achieve a level of refurbishment (act of improvement) in the process of email examination procedure since its launch. Support for forensic disk image format was also added to the application since one of its upgrades. The support is limited only for email storage formats, imaged within the file, owing to the email examination theme of the application. Currently the application is serving legal departments, law enforcement agencies,[10] government sectors, and more such sectors with the requirement of the investigation of email messages.[11]

24.1.1 Key Skills

•Message Rebuilding: Extracts omitted messages from desktop-based email storage formats.

•Detailed Analysis: Serves multiple views for looking into the anatomy of email messages.

•Skin Tone Analysis: Offers detection of obscene / pornographic image media from emails / attachments.[12]

•Court Admissible Output: Generates evidence[13] storage output in court admissible formats.

•Evidence Lookup: Gives away search parameters and types to lookup evidence with accuracy.[14]

•Universal Email Support: Examines email storage for web and desktop based services.

•Comprehensive Reporting: Performs reporting of complete investigation activities.

•Case Management: Builds case repository for collection of correlated / single case email storage.

•Export Restriction Applicable: Offers to apply privilege over emails for evidence export restriction.

Additional improvements are in pipeline and soon to be released in the next possible release.

24.2 See also

- List of Digital Forensics Tools
- Forensic Search
- Computer Forensics

24.3 References

[1] "About Email Examiner". *MailXaminer*. Retrieved July 20, 2015.

[2] "Search for forensic tools by functionality". *Computer Forensics Tool Catalog*. Retrieved July 20, 2015.

[3] Devendran, V. , Shahriar, H. and Clincy, V. (2015) A Comparative Study of Email Forensic Tools. Journal of Information Security, 6, 111-117. doi: 10.4236/jis.2015.62012

[4] "Department of Compute Science, Kennesaw State University, Kennesaw, GA, USA". *SCIRP*. Retrieved July 20, 2015.

[5] "Forensic Email Analysis Software, 'MailXaminer' Available With Key Features". *WhaTech.com*. October 6, 2014. Retrieved July 20, 2015.

[6] "A Framework for Extended Acquisition and Uniform Representation of ForensicEmail Evidence" (PDF). *http://repository.asu.edu"*. *November 2013. Retrieved July 20, 2015.*

[7] Singh, Sudhakar (December 2014). "SysTools Software: Building Innovative Tools for Digital Forensics". *CIOReview*. Retrieved July 20, 2015.

[8] "MailXaminer". *Forensic Magazine*. November 7, 2014. Retrieved July 21, 2015.

[9] "7 Cybersecurity, Forensics Tools to Watch". *Corporate Counsel*. June 24, 2013. Retrieved July 21, 2015.

[10] "Top Law Enforcement Software Products". *Capterra*. May 26, 2015. Retrieved July 21, 2015.

[11] "MailXaminer Webmail Forensic Tool to Extract Emails and Collect Evidences for Proof". *GhanaWeb Blog*. November 6, 2014. Retrieved July 21, 2015.

[12] "SysTools Introduces MailXaminer 4.7, Skin Tool Analysis Feature to Enhance Forensic Investigations". *CIO Review*. November 2014. Retrieved July 21, 2015.

[13] Aswani (January 6, 2015). "How to Search Seized Emails to Obtain Evidence with MailXaminer?". *AksindiBlog*. Retrieved July 21, 2015.

[14] "Digital Forensic Evidence Examination" (PDF). *Meantbooks*. April 2014. Retrieved July 21, 2015.

24.4   External links

- MailXaminer Product page

- forensicswiki MailXaminer

- Software links for Forensics Investigative Tasks

- MailXaminer

Chapter 25

Memory forensics

Memory forensics is forensic analysis of a computer's memory dump. Its primary application is investigation of advanced computer attacks which are stealthy enough to avoid leaving data on the computer's hard drive. Consequently, the memory (RAM) must be analyzed for forensic information.

25.1 History

25.1.1 Zeroth generation tools

Prior to 2004, memory forensics was done on an *ad hoc* basis, using generic data analysis tools like strings and grep. These tools are not specifically created for memory forensics, and therefore are difficult to use. They also provide limited information. In general, their primary usage is to extract text from the memory dump.[1]

Many operating systems provide features to kernel developers and end-users to actually create a snapshot of the physical memory for either debugging (core dump or Blue Screen of Death) purposes or experience enhancement (Hibernation (computing)). In the case of Microsoft Windows, crash dumps and hibernation had been present since Microsoft Windows NT. Microsoft crash dumps had always been analyzable by Microsoft WinDbg, and Windows hibernation files (hiberfil.sys) are nowadays convertible in Microsoft crash dumps using utilities like MoonSols Windows Memory Toolkit designed by Matthieu Suiche.

25.1.2 First generation tools

In February 2004, Michael Ford introduced memory forensics into security investigations with an article in SysAdmin Magazine.[2] In that article, he demonstrated analysis of a memory based rootkit. The process utilized the existing Linux crash utility as well as two tools developed specifically to recover and analyze the memory forensically, memget and mempeek.

In 2005, DFRWS issued a Memory Analysis Forensics Challenge.[3] In response to this challenge, more tools in this generation, specifically designed to analyze memory dumps, were created. These tools had knowledge of the operating system's internal data structures, and were thus capable of reconstructing the operating system's process list and process information.[3]

Although intended as research tools, they proved that operating system level memory forensics is possible and practical.

25.1.3 Second generation tools

Subsequently, several memory forensics tools were developed intended for practical use. These include both commercial tools like Memoryze, MoonSols Windows Memory Toolkit, open source tools like Volatility. New features have been added, such as analysis of Linux and Mac OS X memory dumps, and substantial academic research has been carried out.[4][5]

Unlike Microsoft Windows, Mac OS X interest is relatively new and had only been initiated by Matthieu Suiche[6] in 2010 during Black Hat Briefings security conference.

Currently, memory forensics is a standard component of incident response.[7]

25.1.4 Third generation tools

Since 2010, we started to see more utilities focusing on the visualization aspect of memory analysis such as MoonSols LiveCloudKd presented[8] by Matthieu Suiche at Microsoft BlueHat Security Briefings that inspired[9] a new feature in Microsoft LiveKd written by Mark Russinovich to allow virtual machines introspection by accessing the memory of guest virtual machine from the host virtual machine in order to either analyze them directly with the assistance of Microsoft WinDbg or to acquire a memory dump in a Microsoft crash dump file format.

25.2   References

[1] Dan Farmer and Wietse Venema.*Forensic Discovery*.Chapter 8.

[2] Ford, Michael. (2004) Linux Memory Forensics SysAdmin Magazine.

[3] DFRWS 2005 Forensics Challenge

[4] Petroni, N. L., Walters, A., Fraser, T., & Arbaugh, W. A. (2006). FATKit: A framework for the extraction and analysis of digital forensic data from volatile system memory. Digital Investigation, 3(4), 197-210.

[5] Inoue, H., Adelstein, F., & Joyce, R. A. (2011). Visualization in testing a volatile memory forensic tool. Digital Investigation, 8, S42-S51.

[6] Matthieu Suiche. Black Hat Briefings DC 2010.Advanced Mac OS X Physical Memory Analysis.

[7] SANS Institute. Memory Forensics for Incident Response.

[8] Matthieu Suiche. Microsoft Blue Hat Hacker Conference Fall 2010.Blue Screen of Death is Dead.

[9] LiveKd for Virtual Machines Debugging

Chapter 26

Nuix

Warning: Page using Template:Infobox company with unknown parameter "origins" (this message is shown only in preview).

Nuix Pty Ltd is an Australian company that produces a software platform for indexing, searching, analyzing and extracting knowledge from unstructured data, with applications that include digital investigation, cybersecurity, e-Discovery, information governance, email migration and privacy. The software platform is used by organizations in more than 45 countries.[1]

26.1 History

- In 2014 Nuix was appointed an Industry Partner of the International Multilateral Partnership Against Cyber Threats.[2]

- By April 2014, Nuix had raised more than $146,000 for Room to Read from its philanthropic product Proof Finder.[3] Proof Finder is a sophisticated eDiscovery and investigation software tool which Nuix released in December 2011 as a philanthropic venture.[4]

- In 2012 Nuix won the Information and Communication Technology category of the Australian Export Awards.[5]

- In 2010 Nuix won a five-year contract with the Securities and Exchange Commission.[6]

- In 2009 Nuix won the NSW Australian Technology Showcase (ATS) export award.[7]

- In 2009 Nuix won the NSW Emerging Exporter Award.[8]

26.2 Notable Uses

Nuix donated software licences and training to the International Consortium of Investigative Journalists (ICIJ), who used Nuix to investigate the Offshore Leaks data.[9]

26.3 References

[1] "Interviews - 2014 Jim Kent, CEO EMEA, Nuix". *http://www.forensicfocus.com*. 2014-05-14. Retrieved 2014-05-19. External link in |work= (help)

[2] "Nuix and ITU-IMPACT Partner in Building Capacity to Address Global Cyber Threats". 2014-03-19. Retrieved 2014-04-07.

[3] "The philanthropic software model works, so what are you waiting for?". 2014-03-19. Retrieved 2014-04-07.

[4] "Nuix reached its fundraising target of $100,000 for Room To Read, with sales of Proof Finder.". 2013-07-29. Retrieved 2013-07-29.

[5] "2012 Australian Export Award Winners". 2012-11-27. Retrieved 2012-12-14.

[6] "Nuix on hitting the export jackpot". *zdnet.com.au*. 2010-03-05. Retrieved 2010-09-08.

[7] "Investigation software company wins NSW technology export award". *business.nsw.gov.au*. 2009-10-22. Retrieved 2010-09-08.

[8] "NSW Export Awards Winners". *exportawards.gov.au*. Retrieved 2010-09-08.

[9] "How ICIJ's Project Team Analyzed the Offshore Files". Retrieved 4 May 2013.

26.4 External links

- Official website

Chapter 27

Open Computer Forensics Architecture

The **Open Computer Forensics Architecture** (OCFA) is an distributed open-source computer forensics framework used to analyze digital media within a digital forensics laboratory environment. The framework was built by the Dutch national police.

27.1 Architecture

OCFA consists of a back end for the Linux platform, it uses a PostgreSQL database for data storage, a custom Content-addressable storage or CarvFS based data repository and a Lucene index. The front end for OCFA has not been made publicly available due to licensing issues.

The framework integrates with other open source forensic tools and includes modules for The Sleuth Kit, Scalpel, Photorec, libmagic, GNU Privacy Guard, objdump, exiftags, zip, 7-zip, tar, gzip, bzip2, rar, antiword, qemu-img, and mbx2mbox. OCFA is extensible in C++ or Java.

27.2 See also

- List of digital forensics tools

27.3 External links

- Official website

- Linux Magazine article on OCFA

- Open Source Software for Digital Forensics

Chapter 28

PTK Forensics

PTK Forensics (PTK) was a non-free, commercial GUI for old versions of the digital forensics tool The Sleuth Kit (TSK). It also includes a number of other software modules for investigating digital media. The software is not developed anymore.

PTK runs as a GUI interface for The Sleuth Kit, acquiring and indexing digital media for investigation. Indexes are stored in an SQL database for searching as part of a digital investigation. PTK calculates a hash signature (using SHA-1 and MD5) for acquired media for verification and consistency purposes.[1]

28.1 References

[1] hash set mgmt

28.2 External links

- SourceForge.net download site for PTK

Chapter 29

Registry Recon

Registry Recon is a computer forensics tool that allows users to see how Registries from both current and former installations of Microsoft Windows have changed over time. It was developed by Arsenal Recon, whose slogan is "Computer forensics tools by computer forensics experts." Registry Recon first extracts Registry information from a piece of evidence (disk image, properly mounted slave drive, etc.), whether that information was active, backed up in restore points or Volume Shadow Copies, or deleted. Registry Recon then rebuilds all the Registries represented by the extracted information. Registry Recon was the first (and is currently the only)[1] digital forensics tool to rebuild Registries from both active and previous installations of Windows. The product is named after the French word *reconnaissance* ("recognition"), the military concept of probing unfriendly territory for tactical information.

29.1 Overview

The Windows Registry is a core component of all modern versions of Microsoft Windows. It is a complex ecosystem, in database form, containing information related to hardware, software, and users which is useful to computer forensics practitioners. At a very basic level, the Registry is composed of "keys" and "values" which are similar in some ways to folders and files. The Registry is continually referenced during Windows operation so large volumes of Registry data can be found both on disk and in volatile memory. Registry Recon was designed to address two major shortcomings of existing computer forensics tools - seamlessly recovering as much Registry information as possible from a piece of evidence, and rebuilding it in such a way that the user is able to see how the Registry (or Registries) changed over time.

29.1.1 Capabilities

- **Registry Rebuilding**: Extracted Registry information is used to rebuild Registries ("Recon Registries")

that have existed on a piece of evidence over time

- **Recon View**: Rebuilt Registries are visualized in a manner that allows the user to see unique values by default and all instances of those values if so desired

- **Key History**: Keys and their values can be viewed at particular points in time

- **Recon Reports**: Pre-built reports requested by the computer forensics community

- **Windows Backup Support**: Restore points and Volume Shadow Copies are parsed during evidence ingestion

- **Registry Hive Carving**: Registry hives (complete and partial) are carved and parsed from unallocated (a/k/a deleted) space during evidence ingestion

- **Deleted Key Recovery**: Deleted keys within hives (i.e. keys which are no longer known to their parent) are parsed during evidence ingestion

- **Automatic Decoding**: Obfuscated data, whether ROT13 encrypted and/or simply stored in binary form (e.g. UserAssist keys), is automatically decoded

Additional capabilities and improvements are planned, such as selective data parsing (as opposed to entire images / directories), more automated report features, live memory analysis, and improved search functions.[2] [3] [4] [5] [6]

29.2 See also

- Computer forensics

- Windows registry

58

29.3 References

[1] NIST search for forensic tools by functionality, December 20, 2012

[2] review by Forensic Control, February 15, 2013

[3] CyberSpeak interview with Registry Recon developer February 18, 2013

[4] Law Journal Newsletters September 2013

[5] David Cowen interview with Registry Recon developer from 21:05 to 42:05, March 7, 2014

[6] David Cowen review of Registry Recon September 30, 2014

29.4 External links

- Registry Recon Homepage

- Registry Recon Announcement

Chapter 30

Digital Forensics Framework

Digital Forensics Framework (**DFF**) is computer forensics open-source software. It is used by professionals and non-experts to collect, preserve and reveal digital evidence without compromising systems and data.[2]

30.1 User interfaces

Digital Forensics Framework offers a graphical user interface (GUI) developed in PyQt and a classical tree view. Features such as recursive view, tagging, live search and bookmarking are available. Its command line interface allows the user to remotely perform digital investigation. It comes with common shell functions such as completion, task management, globing and keyboard shortcuts. DFF can run batch scripts at startup to automate repetitive tasks. Advanced users and developers can use DFF directly from a Python interpreter to script their investigation.

30.2 Distribution methods

In addition to the source code package and binary installers for GNU/Linux and Windows,[3] Digital Forensics Framework is available in operating system distributions as is typical in free and open-source software (FOSS), including Debian,[4] Fedora and[5] Ubuntu.

Other Digital Forensics Framework methods available are digital forensics oriented distribution and live cd:

- DEFT Linux Live CD[6]

- Kali Linux[7]

30.3 Publications

- "Scriptez vos analyses forensiques avec Python et DFF" in the French magazine MISC[8]

- Several presentations about DFF in conferences: "Digital Forensics Framework" at ESGI Security Day[9] "An introduction to digital forensics" at RMLL 2013[10]

Published books that mention Digital Forensics Framework are:

- Digital Forensics with Open Source Tools (Syngress, 2011)[11]

- Computer Forensik Hacks (O'Reilly, 2012)[12]

- Malwares - Identification, analyse et éradication (Epsilon, 2013)[13]

- Digital Forensics for Handheld Devices (CRC Press Inc, 2012)[14]

30.3.1 In literature

- Saving Rain: The First Novel in The Rain Trilogy[15]

'Erik gives her another appreciative once over before handing her a laptop and turning all business minded. "We've been using the Digital Forensics Framework, ran various algorithms, including k-means clustering, but we keep coming up empty." "What about SSH, cryptographic algorithms?" Raina asks ...'

30.3.2 White papers

- Selective Imaging Revisited[16]

- A survey of main memory acquisition and analysis techniques for the windows operating system[17]

- Uforia : Universal forensic indexer and analyzer[18]

- Visualizing Indicators of Rootkit Infections in Memory Forensics[19]

- EM-DMKM Case Study Computer and Network Forensics[20]

- OV-chipcard DFF Extension[21]

- L'investigation numérique « libre »[22]

- Malware analysis method based on reverse technology (□□ □□□□□□ □)[23]

30.4 Prize

DFF was used to solve the 2010 Digital Forensic Research Workshop (DFRWS) challenge consisting of the reconstructing a physical dump of a NAND flash memory.[24]

30.5 References

[1] "[dff] Digital Forensics Framework 1.3.0 released". Lists.digital-forensic.org. Retrieved 2014-02-16.

[2] "Welcome to S.B. Jain Institute of Technology Management and Research". ArxSys. Retrieved 28 May 2014.

[3] "Open Source digital forensics & incident response software". Digital-forensic.org. Retrieved 2014-02-16.

[4] "DFF accepted into Debian - Pollux's blog". Wzdftpd.net. Retrieved 2014-02-16.

[5]

[6] "DEFT 8 Roadmap and features | DEFT Linux - Computer Forensics live CD". DEFT Linux. Retrieved 2014-02-16.

[7] "Packages Summary". Git.kali.org. 2013-02-02. Retrieved 2014-02-16.

[8] "Misc 70 - LES EDITIONS DIAMOND". Boutique.ed-diamond.com. Retrieved 2014-02-16.

[9]

[10]

[11] "Digital Forensics with Open Source Tools: Cory Altheide, Harlan Carvey: 9781597495868: Amazon.com: Books". Amazon.com. Retrieved 2014-02-16.

[12] "Computer-Forensik Hacks: Amazon.de: Lorenz Kuhlee, Victor Völzow: Bücher". Amazon.de. 2009-09-09. Retrieved 2014-02-16.

[13] "Malwares - Identification, analyse et éradication: Amazon.fr: Paul Rascagneres: Livres". Amazon.fr. 2009-09-09. Retrieved 2014-02-16.

[14] "Digital Forensics for Handheld Devices: Amazon.fr: Eamon P. Doherty: Livres anglais et étrangers". Amazon.fr. 2009-09-09. Retrieved 2014-02-16.

[15] "Saving Rain: The First Novel in The Rain Trilogy eBook: Karen-Anne Stewart: Kindle Store". Amazon.com. Retrieved 2014-02-16.

[16] "IEEE Xplore Abstract - Selective Imaging Revisited". Ieeexplore.ieee.org. 2013-03-14. doi:10.1109/IMF.2013.16. Retrieved 2014-02-16.

[17] "A survey of main memory acquisition and analysis techniques for the windows operating system". *Digital Investigation* (Sciencedirect.com) **8**: 3–22. 2011-07-31. doi:10.1016/j.diin.2011.06.002. Retrieved 2014-02-16.

[18] "Uforia: Universal forensic indexer and analyzer - Springer". Link.springer.com. Retrieved 2014-02-16.

[19] "IEEE Xplore Abstract - Visualizing Indicators of Rootkit Infections in Memory Forensics". Ieeexplore.ieee.org. 2013-03-14. doi:10.1109/IMF.2013.12. Retrieved 2014-02-16.

[20] "EM-DMKM Case Study Computer and Network Forensics" (PDF). Cygalski.pl. Retrieved 2014-02-16.

[21]

[22] "L'investigation numerique" (PDF) (in French). Agence-nationale-recherche.fr. Retrieved 2014-02-16.

[23] "Journal of Computer Applications : Vol.31 No.11". Joca.cn. November 2011. Retrieved 2014-02-16.

[24] "DFRWS 2010 Forensics Challenge Results". Dfrws.org. Retrieved 2014-02-16.

30.6 External links

- Official website

- Digital Forensics Framework Wiki

Chapter 31

SANS Investigative Forensics Toolkit

The **SANS Investigative Forensic Toolkit ("SIFT")** is a computer forensics VMware appliance that is pre-configured with all the necessary tools to perform a detailed digital forensic examination. It is compatible with expert witness format (E01), advanced forensic format (AFF), and raw (dd) evidence formats. The new version has been completely rebuilt on an Ubuntu base with many additional tools and capabilities that can match any modern forensic tool suite.

31.1 Use

The toolkit has the ability to securely examine raw disks, multiple file systems, and evidence formats. It places strict guidelines on how evidence is examined (read-only), verifying that the evidence has not changed.

31.1.1 File system support

- Windows (MS-DOS, FAT, VFAT, NTFS)
- Mac (HFS)
- Solaris (UFS)
- Linux (ext2/3)

31.1.2 Evidence image support

- Expert Witness (E01/L01)
- RAW (dd)
- Advanced Forensic Format (AFF)

31.1.3 Software

- MantaRay (Automated Forensic Processing), MantaRay's GitHub

- The Sleuth Kit (File system analysis tools)
- log2timeline (timeline generation tool)
- ssdeep & md5deep (hashing tools)
- Foremost/Scalpel (File Carving)
- Wireshark (Network Forensics)
- Vinetto (thumbs.db examination)
- Pasco (IE Web History examination)
- Rifiuti (Recycle Bin examination)
- Volatility Framework (memory analysis)
- DFLabs PTK (GUI front-end for Sleuthkit)
- Autopsy (GUI front-end for Sleuthkit)
- PyFLAG (GUI Log/Disk examination)

31.2 References

31.3 Further reading

31.4 External links

- SANS Digital Forensics and Incident Response web site

Chapter 32

SecurityMetrics

SecurityMetrics is a multinational merchant data security and compliance company headquartered in Orem, Utah.[2] The company is a Payment Card Industry (PCI) Data Security Standard (DSS) vendor, listed[3] as a Qualified Security Assessor (QSA), Approved Scanning Vendor (ASV), P2PE QSA, PCI Forensic Investigator (PFI) and Payment Application Qualified Security Assessor (PA-QSA) by the PCI Security Standards Council.[4] SecurityMetrics has working relationships with major payment processing companies and global acquiring banks such as Global Payments Inc, Sterling Payment Technologies, and FirstMerit Bank to provide PCI compliance and other security solutions to their merchants.[5] SecurityMetrics currently has the largest support staff in the PCI industry worldwide, fielding over 132,000 calls a month, and employs nearly 400 employees.[6]

SecurityMetrics has been an A+ accredited business through the Better Business Bureau (BBB) since May 2005.[7]

32.1 Product History

SecurityMetrics was founded in 2000 by Brad Caldwell with the goal to test website security.[8] In 2002, SecurityMetrics released its first vulnerability scanning appliance. In 2003 SecurityMetrics released its first hardware device with intrusion detection and vulnerability assessment technology, and conducted its first forensic investigation.

SecurityMetrics was officially named a QSA and ASV by the PCI Council in 2006,[9] and certified as a security assessor for all four major card associations in the United States: Visa, MasterCard, American Express, and Discover.

In 2008, SecurityMetrics hit the 1 million customer mark and in 2009 the company was officially named a PA-QSA by the PCI Council. In 2010 it released PANscan®,[10] a card data discovery tool. In 2011 the company released a network threat sensor called Vision.

In 2012, SecurityMetrics released a breach protection service intended to help back its users in the event of a compromise with a $100,000 reimbursement for breach expenses.[11] SecurityMetrics also released its new PCI verification and testing program, PCI Focus.

In 2013, SecurityMetrics released a Health Insurance Portability and Accountability Act compliance assessment program[12] intended to assist covered entity healthcare organizations in complying with HIPAA Security and Omnibus Final Rule[13] regulations. In May the company also announced an iOS and Android [14][15] app called MobileScan [16] intended to scan payment processing phones and tablets for security vulnerabilities.

In 2015, SecurityMetrics released its HIPAA compliance dashboard[17] that stores the results of a HIPAA risk analysis, risk management plan, and documentation for HIPAA training, and policies in one place.

32.2 Awards

Security Metrics have been awarded several industry awards including multiple Stevie Awards for Sales and Customer Service,[18] and local Utah awards for business and entrepreneurship.

32.3 References

[1] Management - SecurityMetrics (accessed 6 December 2012)

[2] About Us - SecurityMetrics (accessed 6 December 2012)

[3] PCI DSS Listed Qualified Security Assessors (accessed 27 September 2011)

[4] Qualified Security Assessors (accessed 5 August 2010)

[5] ISO Launches PCI Compliance Program, Sees Strong Interest Among Merchants (accessed 17 August 20100

[6] Global Payments Inc. - PCI DSS Program (accessed 25 August 2010)

[7] SecurityMetrics, Inc. -BBB (accessed 5 July 2011)

[8] Orem, Utah open house speech, Brad Caldwell] (accessed 31 August 2011)

[9] Company passes PCI SSC Approved Scanning Vendor (ASV) test (accessed 29 August 2012)

[10] Despite PCI, a Scanning Tool Finds Widespread Storage of Unencrypted Data (accessed 29 August 2012)

[11] SecurityMetrics Assurance Empowers Acquirers, ISOs to Operate Without Fear of Merchant Compromise (accessed 29 August 2012)

[12] About SecurityMetrics HIPAA (accessed 29 August 2012)

[13] HHS Omnibus Final Rule Press Release

[14] iOS app (accessed 28 August 2013)

[15] Android app (accessed 28 August 2013)

[16] (accessed 9 May 2013)

[17] Press Release: One-Stop HIPAA Dashboard Helps Complete and Document All Requirements (accessed 11 August 2015)

[18] 2013 Stevie Award Winners (accessed 4 April 2013)

32.4   External links

- SecurityMetrics

Chapter 33

Selective file dumper

Selective File Dumper (SFDumper) is a free open source computer forensics tool, written by Nanni Bassetti and Denis Frati, for Linux systems.

It is a Bash script which can retrieve all the files of a chosen type (e.g. .doc or .jpg), regardless if they are active, deleted or unallocated. It automatically runs Foremost for carving, and Sleuthkit for deleted files retrieval. It then eliminates duplicated files by comparing the SHA256 hashes of the carved files and the active and deleted files. Thanks to carving, files simply renamed to a different extension will be identified. Also, it is possible to expand the Foremost configuration file inside the script to add new extensions. Finally, it is possible to do a keyword search on the extracted files. The script can work on an image file or directly from a device.

It is free software licensed under the terms of the GNU General Public License (GPL) and GNU Lesser General Public License (LGPL).

33.1 Requirements

- Linux OS
- Sleuthkit
- Foremost
- Sha256deep
- grep
- awk
- sed
- dd

33.1.1 Requirements for the GUI version

- Zenity

33.2 External links

- http://sfdumper.sourceforge.net/
- http://www.caine-live.net

Chapter 34

The Sleuth Kit

The Sleuth Kit (**TSK**) is a library and collection of Unix- and Windows-based tools and utilities to allow for the forensic analysis of computer systems. It was written and maintained by digital investigator Brian Carrier. TSK can be used to perform investigations and data extraction from images of Windows, Linux and Unix computers. The Sleuth Kit is normally used in conjunction with its custom frontend application, Autopsy, to provide a user friendly interface. Several other tools also use TSK for file extraction.

The Sleuth Kit is a free, open source suite that provides a large number of specialized command-line based utilities.

It is based on The Coroner's Toolkit, and is the official successor platform.[1]

34.1 Tools

Some of the tools included in The Sleuth Kit include:

- **ils** lists all metadata entries, such as an Inode.

- **blkls** displays data blocks within a file system (formerly called dls).

- **fls** lists allocated and unallocated file names within a file system.

- **fsstat** displays file system statistical information about an image or storage medium.

- **ffind** searches for file names that point to a specified metadata entry.

- **mactime** creates a timeline of all files based upon their MAC times.

- **disk_stat** (currently Linux-only) discovers the existence of a Host Protected Area.

34.2 See also

- Selective file dumper

- The Coroner's Toolkit

- Autopsy (software)—A graphical user interface wrapped around The Sleuth Kit.

34.3 References

[1] http://www.porcupine.org/forensics/tct.html

34.4 External links

- The Sleuth Kit Official website

- The Sleuth Kit Informer newsletter

- Sleuth Kit Wiki

Chapter 35

StegAlyzerAS

Steganography Analyzer Artifact Scanner, or StegAlyzerAS, is a computer forensics software made by Backbone Security's Steganography Analysis and Research Center. It is designed to extend the scope of traditional digital forensic examinations by allowing the examiner to scan suspect media or forensic images of suspect media for known artifacts of steganography applications.[1]

Artifacts may be identified by scanning the file system as well as the registry on a Microsoft Windows system. StegAlyzerAS allows for identification of files by using CRC-32, MD5, SHA-1, SHA-224, SHA-256, SHA-384, and SHA-512 hash values stored in the Steganography Application Fingerprint Database (SAFDB). SAFDB is the largest commercially available steganography hash set.[2] Known registry keys are identified by using the Registry Artifact Key Database (RAKDB) distributed with StegAlyzerAS.

35.1 References

[1] "TUCOFS - The Ultimate Collection of Forensic Software".

[2] "Backbone Security is pleased to announce the release of Version 3.9 of the Steganography Application Fingerprint Database".

35.2 External links

- Steganography Analyzer Artifact Scanner

Chapter 36

Trend Micro

Trend Micro Inc. (Japanese: 🔲🔲🔲🔲🔲🔲🔲🔲🔲🔲🔲 Torendo Maikuro Kabushiki-Gaisha; Chinese: 🔲🔲🔲) is a global security software company founded in Los Angeles, California with global headquarters in Tokyo, Japan, and regional headquarters in Asia, Europe and the Americas. The company develops security software for servers, cloud computing environments, and small business. Its cloud and virtualization security products provide cloud security for customers of VMware,[2] Amazon AWS,[3] Microsoft Azure[4] and vCloud Air. Eva Chen serves as Trend Micro's chief executive officer, a position she has held since 2005 when she succeeded founding CEO Steve Chang. Chang serves as chairman of Trend Micro.[5]

36.1 History

The company was founded in 1988 in Los Angeles by Steve Chang (🔲🔲🔲, Chang Ming-cheng), his wife, Jenny Chang, and her sister, Eva Chen (🔲🔲🔲).[6] The company was established with proceeds from Steve Chang's previous sale of a copy protection dongle to a United States-based Rainbow Technologies.[7] Shortly after establishing the company, its founders moved headquarters to Taipei.[8]

In 1992, Trend Micro took over a Japanese software firm to form Trend Micro Devices and established headquarters in Japan. It then made an agreement with CPU maker Intel under which it produced an anti-virus product for local area networks (LANs) for sale under the Intel brand. Intel paid royalties to Trend Micro for sales of LANDesk Virus Protect in the United States and Europe, while Trend paid royalties to Intel for sales in Asia. In 1993, Novell began bundling the product with its network operating system.[8] In 1996 the two companies agreed to a two-year continuation of the agreement in which Trend was allowed to globally market the ServerProtect product under its own brand alongside Intel's LANDesk brand.

Trend Micro was listed on the Tokyo Stock Exchange in 1998 under the ticker 4704.[7] The company began trading on the United States-based NASDAQ stock exchange in July 1999.[9]

In 2004, founding chief executive officer Steve Chang decided to split the responsibilities of CEO and chairman of the company.[7] Company co-founder Eva Chen succeeded Steve Chang as chief executive officer of Trend Micro in January 2005.[5] Chen had most recently served as the company's chief technology officer since 1996 and before that executive vice president since the company's founding in May 1988.[5] Steve Chang retained his position as company chairman.[5] In May, Trend Micro acquired Braintree, Massachusetts-based antispyware company InterMute for $15 million.[10] Trend Micro had fully integrated InterMute's SpySubtract antispyware program into its antispyware product offerings by the end of that year.[10][11] In June 2005 Trend Micro acquired Kelkea, a San Jose, California-based developer of antispam software.[12] Kelkea developed Mail Abuse Prevention System (MAPS) and IP filtering software that allowed internet service providers to block spam and phishing scams.[13] Kelkea chief executive officer Dave Rand was retained by Trend Micro as its chief technologist for content security.[12]

In March 2007, Trend Micro acquired freeware antispyware program HijackThis from its creator Merijn Bellekom for an undisclosed sum.[14][15] Trend Micro delisted its depository shares from the NASDAQ stock exchange in May.[16] Later that year, in October, Trend Micro acquired Mountain View, California-based data loss prevention software developer Provilla.[17] Provilla was the creator LeakProof, software that allowed companies to block the transmission of sensitive data and warn security managers about transmission attempts.[17]

Trend Micro acquired Identum in February 2008 for an undisclosed sum.[18] Identum, which was founded in and later spun-off from the University of Bristol cryptography department, developed ID-based email encryption software.[18] The two companies were originally in talks for Trend Micro to license Identum's technology, but Trend Micro later decided to purchase the firm outright.[18] Identum was renamed Trend Micro (Bristol) and its encryption technology was integrated into existing Trend Micro products.[19] Existing Identum products were continued but sold under the Trend Micro brand.[19] Also that year, Trend Micro sued Barracuda Networks for the latter's distribution of ClamAV as part of a security package.[20] Trend Micro claimed that Barracuda's use of ClamAV infringed on a software patent owned by Trend Micro for filtering viruses on an Internet gateway.[20] On May 19, 2011, the U.S. Patent and Trademark Office issued a Final Rejection[21] in the reexamination of Trend Micro's U.S. patent 5,623,600.[22]

In April 2009, Trend Micro acquired Ottawa, Ontario Canada-based Third Brigade for an undisclosed sum.[23] Third Brigade developed host-based intrusion prevention and firewall software that had been used by Trend Micro in its Trend OfficeScan anti-malware suite for two years prior to acquiring Third Brigade.[23] Third Brigade was reincorporated as Trend Micro Canada Technologies.[24]

Trend Micro acquired Leeds, England-based humyo in June 2010 for an undisclosed sum.[25] humyo provided cloud-based data storage and synchronization services to small businesses and individuals.[25][26] Later that year, in November, Trend Micro acquired Mobile Armor. Mobile Armor was a developer of full disk, file and folder, and removable media encryption for mobile devices.[27] Trend Micro integrated the company's technology into a centrally-managed platform for mobile device security.[27]

In June 2012, Trend Micro acquired Marlborough, Massachusetts-based Secure Sockets Layer (SSL) certificate provider AffirmTrust for an undisclosed sum.[28] Trend Micro followed up with another acquisition, Taiwanese advanced network security firm Broadweb, in October 2012.[29] Broadweb was a developer of deep packet inspection technology that had the ability to block malicious data packets in real-time.[29] The technology was integrated into Trend Micro's Custom Defense Solution, a suite that was designed to provide network-wide visibility and protection against advanced attacks and threats.[30]

Trend Micro relocated its US headquarters to the Las Colinas area of Irving, Texas in September 2013.[28] The relocation allowed the company to consolidate operations previously housed in Cupertino, California and Arlington, Texas.[28][31]

In September 2014, Trend Micro began a three-year partnership with INTERPOL wherein Trend Micro shared with the international police organization information on cybercrime threats via the company's Threat Intelligence Service. According to INTERPOL, the information helped the international police organization and its 190 member countries decrease cybercrime on a global scale. Trend Micro also provided a cybercrime investigation training program to INTERPOL.[32]

In October 2015, Trend Micro reached an agreement to buy TippingPoint, a network and software security developer from HP Inc. for $300 million.[33]

36.2 Products

36.2.1 Consumer products

Trend Micro provides multiple security programs for consumers, including Trend Micro Antivirus+ Security, Trend Micro Internet Security, Trend Micro Maximum Security, Trend Micro Premium Security, and Trend Micro Antivirus for Mac. Additional tools available to consumers included Trend Micro SafeSync (no longer available from February 2016 [34]) for backing up and syncing data between computers and mobile devices and Password Manager, which allows users to manage passwords and login IDs.[35]

Trend Micro also offers security software for mobile devices, including Mobile Security & Antivirus for Android, Mobile Security & Antivirus for iOS, Trend Micro Mobile Security for Kindle, Trend Micro Password Manager for Android, Trend Micro Password Manager for iOS, Smart Surfing for iPhone and SafeSync Mobile.[35]

36.2.2 Small business products

Trend Micro offers Worry-Free Business Security Standard and Advanced on-premises security suites for small businesses. The company also provides for small businesses Worry-Free Business Security Services, a cloud-based security suite hosted by Trend Micro, and InterScan Messaging Hosted Security.[36]

36.2.3 Enterprise and medium business products

Trend Micro Enterprise products offer comprehensive protection from the endpoint and mobile devices to servers, datacenter, network and the cloud. Products offered by Trend Micro Enterprise include OfficeScan, Deep Security, Deep Discovery, InterScan Web Security, InterScan Web Security as a Service, InterScan Messaging Security, ScanMail for Microsoft Exchange, and ServerProtect.[37]

36.2.4 Free tools

Trend Micro acquired the OSSEC project along with its acquisition of Third Brigade, and has promised to keep it open source and free.[38] The company also maintains multiple free security tools, including Browser Guard, HijackThis, HouseCall, Dr. Cleaner for Mac, RootkitBuster, RUBotted, Smart Surfing for iPhone, and Threat Resource Center.[39]

HouseCall

HouseCall, a free web-based utility, scans for and cleans computers of viruses, Trojans, spyware, and other malware. It performs additional security checks to identify and fix vulnerabilities to prevent reinfection. According to Trend Micro, HouseCall is compatible with all browsers and with the following operating systems: Windows XP (32-bit) Home or Professional; Windows Vista (32-bit, 64-bit) Ultimate, Business, Home Premium, or Home Basic; and Windows 7, RC (32-bit, 64-bit); and Windows 8. HouseCall version 7.1 allowed users to perform a Full Scan, Quick Scan, or Custom Scan.[40]

HijackThis

HijackThis is a freeware open source anti-malware application for Microsoft Windows. It scans a user's hard drive and registry for irregularities in Windows installations.[41] Experienced users can review the log files generated by HijackThis to fix security threats.[42]

36.3 Technologies

In June 2008, Trend Micro introduced Trend Micro Smart Protection Network, a cloud-client content security infrastructure that delivers global threat intelligence to protect customers from online threats, such as data stealing malware, phishing attacks, and other web, email, and mobile threats. In 2012, Trend Micro added big data analytics to its Smart Protection Network.[43] Big data analytics allow the network to use behavioral-based identification methods to identify new security threats.[43] The network also combines in-the-cloud technologies with other client-based antivirus technologies to reduce dependency on conventional pattern file downloads on the endpoint.[44] Threat information from Trend Micro's Smart Protection Network is deployed in real time to the company's security software portfolio.[45]

Trend Micro receives its threat intelligence from TrendLabs, the company's research, development, and support center. TrendLabs has ten labs worldwide, and is headquartered in the Philippines and employs 1,200 security experts and engineers.[46] The company's Singapore-based lab provides malware forensics and analysis.[47]

36.4 See also

- Cloud security

- Comparison of antivirus software

- Comparison of computer viruses

36.5 References

[1] "2014 Financial Data" (PDF). Trend Micro. 2015-02-19.

[2] Eduard Kovacs (27 August 2013). "Trend Micro Teams Up with VMware Deep Security Integrated with VMware NSX". *Softpedia*. Retrieved 15 March 2015.

[3] Ellen Messmer (25 June 2014). "Gartner: Best practices for Amazon AWS security". *Network World*. Retrieved 15 March 2015.

[4] Eduard Kovacs (13 May 2014). "Trend Micro and Microsoft Expand Partnership to Provide Security to Azure Customers". *Softpedia*. Retrieved 15 March 2015.

[5] "Trend Micro". *South China Morning Post*. 23 November 2004.

[6] Naomi Nishihara (11 August 2015). "In cybersecurity, workers must think on feet, culture czar says". *The Dallas Morning News*. Retrieved 12 May 2015.

[7] M.L. Cohen (2009). "Trend Micro Inc.". In Jay P. Pederson. *International Directory of Company Histories* **97**. St. James Press. pp. 429–432.

[8] Eugenia Yun (July 2001). "Hard Sell for Software". Retrieved 15 March 2015.

[9] "New Stock Listings". *The Wall Street Journal*. 12 July 1999.

[10] Hiawatha Bray (11 May 2005). "Japanese Firm to Buy Braintree's Intermute for $1.5M". *The Boston Globe*.

[11] Jack Kapica (31 October 2005). "Trend Micro steps up fight against hackers". *The Globe and Mail*.

[12] "Trend Micro tackles spam with Kelkea buy; The antivirus company's purchase of Kelkea beefs up its spam credentials and sets it on the road to tackling phishing.". *CNET*. 14 June 2005.

[13] "News bits". *Network World*. 20 June 2005.

[14] Neil J. Rubenking (13 March 2007). "Free HijackThis Tool Acquired by Trend Micro". *PC Magazine*.

[15] Ellen Messmer (14 March 2007). "Trend Micro acquires HijackThis antispyware; HijackThis to remain as freeware for public use". *Network World Fusion*.

[16] "Trend Micro Notice Regarding Completion of Delisting of Its ADRs from NASDAQ" (Press release). PR Newswire Asia. 1 June 2007.

[17] Ellen Messmer (25 October 2007). "Trned Micro buys data=leak specialist Provilla". *Network World Fusion*.

[18] "Data spy-beater sold to us rival". *Bristol Evening Post*. 28 February 2008.

[19] "Trend Micro Purchases Identum for Identity-Based Email Encryption". *Wireless News* (Press release). 1 March 2008.

[20] Extremetech Staff (29 January 2008). "Update: Barracuda Takes on Trend Micro over ClamAV Patents". *PC Magazine*. Retrieved 15 March 2015.

[21] "Ex Parte Reexamination" (PDF). U.S. Patent and Trademark Office. 2011-05-19. Retrieved 2015-10-04.

[22] "Anatomy of a Dying Patent - The Reexamination of Trend Micro's '600 Patent". Groklaw.net. 2011-06-13. Retrieved 2015-10-04.

[23] Ellen Messmer (29 April 2009). "UPDATE: Trend Micro acquiring Third Brigade as part of data-center security strategy". *Network World*. Retrieved 15 March 2015.

[24] Rafael Ruffolo (29 April 2009). "Trned Mciro buys Third Brigade, gains Canadian presence". *IT World Canada*. Retrieved 15 March 2015.

[25] Lance Whitney (14 June 2010). "Trend Micro to buy cloud storage provider Humyo". *CNET*. Retrieved 15 March 2015.

[26] Chris Mellor (14 June 2010). "Trend Micro lays down bread for humyo cloud service". *The Register*. Retrieved 15 March 2015.

[27] Tony Bradley (29 November 2010). "Trend Micro Boosts Data Protection with Mobile Armor Purchase". *PC World*. Retrieved 15 March 2015.

[28] Don Seiffert (27 June 2012). "AffirmTrust acquired by billion-dollar Japanese company". *Boston Business Journal*. Retrieved 15 March 2015.

[29] Charlie Osbrone (10 October 2013). "Trend Micro acquires advanced persistent threat defender Broadweb". *ZDNet*. Retrieved 15 March 2015.

[30] Tina Costanza (10 November 2013). "Trend Micro to enhance networks' protection with Broadweb acquisition". *Silicon Republic*. Retrieved 15 March 2015.

[31] "Trend Micro Opens New Global Operations Headquarters". *Security Week*. 18 September 2013. Retrieved 15 March 2015.

[32] Leon Spencer (1 October 2014). "Trend Micro to share threat information with Interpol". *ZDNet*. Retrieved 15 March 2015.

[33] Osborne, Charlie (October 21, 2015). "Trend Micro Acquires HP's TippingPoint security team in $300 Million Deal". ZD Net. Retrieved November 25, 2015.

[34] "Trend Safesync End of Life". Trend Micro. Retrieved 15 March 2015.

[35] "All Products and Free Trials". Trend Micro. Retrieved 15 March 2015.

[36] "All Products and Free Trials". Trend Micro. Retrieved 15 March 2015.

[37] "All Products and Free Trials". Trend Micro. Retrieved 15 March 2015.

[38] "Trend Micro to Acquire Third Brigade". 29 April 2009. Archived from the original on 29 June 2009. Retrieved 15 March 2015.

[39] "All Products and Free Trials". Trend Micro. Retrieved 15 March 2015.

[40] Compare: Sally Wiener Grotta (13 February 2010). "Trend Micro HouseCall Helps Find and desplay Destroy Malware". *PC World*. Retrieved 2015-09-27. You can choose to do a Quick Scan, Full Scan or Custom Scan (choosing which drives and folders-- including connected network drives-- will be analyzed).

[41] Jon L. Jacobi (9 May 2012). "Stop Spyware in Its Tracks With Open-Source HijackThis". *PC World*. Retrieved 15 March 2015.

[42] "Trend Micro HijackThis". CNET. 1 October 2014. Retrieved 15 March 2015.

[43] Fahmida Y. Rashid (7 August 2012). "Trend Micro Adds Big Data Capabilities to its "Smart Protection Network" for Enhanced Cloud, Mobile and Targeted Attack Protection". *SecurityWeek*. Retrieved 15 March 2015.

[44] Stefanie Hoffman (18 June 2008). "Trend Micro Releases New 'Smart Protection Network'". *CRN*. Archived from the original on 24 September 2010. Retrieved 15 March 2015.

[45] Ellen Messmer (6 August 2012). "Trend Micro package protects against unpatched exploits". *Network World*. Retrieved 15 March 2015.

[46] "PH is hub of technology giant". *Manila Standard Today*. 3 February 2013. Retrieved 15 March 2015.

[47] Ellyne Phneah (21 August 2013). "Trned Micro establishes forensics research lab in S'pore". *ZDNet*. Retrieved 15 March 2015.

36.6 External links

- Official website

- TrendWatch Threat Resource Center

- HouseCall

- Malware Blog

- Trend Cloud Security Blog

- Threat Encyclopedia

- Trend Micro Smart Protection Network

Chapter 37

VMRay

VMRay is a German CyberSecurity company based in Bochum, Germany. The company provides both a cloud-based and on-premises product, VMRay Analyzer, for detection of malware using dynamic program analysis. VMRay uses hypervisor-based monitoring built on the academic work of the two founders. VMRay Analyzer is primarily used by CERTs and SOCs in large enterprises, telecoms and other technology vendors for identifying malware, in particular targeted attacks related to APTs

37.1 History

VMRay was founded by Carsten Willems and Ralf Hund in 2013 based on the work each had done as part of their Ph.Ds[1] they received that year in computer science / IT-security at the Ruhr-University of Bochum. The first production deployment of VMRay technology was in early 2015. This technology was in turn built on their earlier work on automating dynamic malware analysis.[2] VMRay has received funding from High-Tech Gruenderfonds[3]

37.2 Product

- VMRay Analyzer is an agentless hypervisor-based software or cloud service that monitors and dynamically analyzes suspicious files and URLs and scores the severity of maliciousness based on the analyzed behavior.

37.3 References

[1] : Hypervisor-based, hardware-assisted system monitoring C Willems, R Hund, T Holz - Ruhr-Universitat Bochum, Tech. Rep, 2013 Cxpinspector

[2] : Toward Automated Dynamic Malware Analysis Using CWSandbox C Willems, Felix Freiling, T Holz - IEEE Security & Privacy, vol.5, no. 2, pp. 32-39, March/April 2007, doi:10.1109/MSP.2007.45 cwsandbox

[3] "High-Tech Gruenderfonds Invests in the Next-Generation Malware Analysis Software of VMRay GmbH". *VC-startups*.

-

37.4 External links

- Official website

Chapter 38

Volatility (memory forensics)

Volatility is an open source memory forensics framework for incident response and malware analysis. It is written in Python and supports Microsoft Windows, OS X, and Linux (as of version 2.4[1]).

Volatility was created by computer scientist and entrepreneur Aaron Walters, drawing on academic research he did in memory forensics.[2][3]

38.1   References

[1] http://www.volatilityfoundation.org/#!24/c12wa

[2] Petroni, N. L., Walters, A., Fraser, T., & Arbaugh, W. A. (2006). *FATKit: A framework for the extraction and analysis of digital forensic data from volatile system memory.* Digital Investigation, 3(4), 197-210.

[3] Walters, A., & Petroni, N. L. (2007). Volatools: Integrating Volatile Memory into the Digital Investigation Process. Black Hat Briefings DC 2007, 1-18.

Chapter 39

WindowsSCOPE

WindowsSCOPE is a memory forensics and reverse engineering product for Windows used for acquiring and analyzing volatile memory.[1] One of its uses is in the detection and reverse engineering of rootkits and other malware.[2]

39.1 Acquisition

WindowsSCOPE supports both software-based acquisition as well as hardware-assisted methods for both locked and unlocked computers. WindowsSCOPE add-on hardware for memory acquisition uses the PCI Express bus for direct access to system memory. Memory snapshots acquired with WindowsSCOPE are stored in a repository. Memory snapshots in the repository can be compared to track changes in the system over time.[2]

39.2 Analysis

WindowsSCOPE shows Processes, DLLs, and drivers running the computer at the time of the memory snapshot as well as open network sockets, file handles, and registry key handles. It also provides disassembly and control flow graphing for executable code. WindowsSCOPE Live is a version of the tool that allows analysis to be performed from a mobile device.[3]

39.3 References

[1] Klanke, Russ. "Digital Forensics Links". *Aggressive Virus Defense*. Retrieved 10 April 2012.

[2] Le Masle, Adrien. "Detecting the HackerDefender rootkit using WindowsSCOPE". Imperial College London. Retrieved 10 April 2012.

[3] Storm, Darlene. "Encrypt: Be anti-forensic friendly to protect your Android and your privacy". *Security Is Sexy*. Computerworld. Retrieved 10 April 2012.

39.4 External links

- WindowsSCOPE Web Site

39.5 Text and image sources, contributors, and licenses

39.5.1 Text

- **Computer forensics** *Source:* https://en.wikipedia.org/wiki/Computer_forensics?oldid=704678485 *Contributors:* The Anome, Comte0, Jimregan, GCarty, Dcoetzee, Ww, AC, Tero~enwiki, Joy, Bloodshedder, Jerzy, Aluion, Phil Boswell, Bearcat, Robbot, Merovingian, Texture, Centrx, DocWatson42, Binarygal, Mboverload, Pascal666, ALargeElk, Wmahan, Necrothesp, DanielCD, Rich Farmbrough, ArnoldReinhold, Bender235, CanisRufus, El C, Krellis, Justinc, Apoc2400, Mrmiscellanious~enwiki, Jgfoot, Randy Johnston, MSR~enwiki, Ceyockey, Mahanga, Bobrayner, Mindmatrix, Thorbjørn Ellefsen, Simsong, Matilda, Kbdank71, Dave Cohoe, Honeyjew, Rjwilmsi, Tizio, PinchasC, Ligulem, G Clark, Nivix, Intgr, Epitome83, Chobot, GroupOne, YurikBot, Wavelength, Borgx, Splintercellguy, Gene.arboit, Wimt, Sanguinity, B-Con, Janke, Arichnad, AlMac, Długosz, Thiseye, BirgitteSB, Mmmbeer, Orbframe, Avraham, 21655, Zzuuzz, Abune, Th1rt3en, Smoshlak, Modify, Dspradau, GraemeL, Rurik, Speisert, Dontaskme, Jessekornblum, Algae, SmackBot, Mmernex, Reedy, Gilliam, Chris the speller, TimBentley, SchfiftyThree, Xx236, Frap, JonHarder, Afcyrus, Midnightcomm, Khoikhoi, Radagast83, Dreadstar, Newsmare, Vina-iwbot~enwiki, Praveen Dalal, Krashlandon, Rklawton, Kuru, Alistair.phillips1, Robert Bond, Khanssen, Waggers, Webucation, Asyndeton, Andreworkney, Hu12, Webmaster961, Gajedi, Freber1977, Igoldste, Blehfu, Dancontiki, Rattatosk, Peterb323, Ghaly, CmdrObot, Ron Barker, Random name, Moreschi, Chris83, Pseudo clever, Cydebot, Amars, Variables, Gogo Dodo, Nabokov, ErrantX, Nuwewsco, DGX, Vmanoussos, TimVickers, Cinnamon42, Cloizides mmacnicol, Cappleby-dborkowski, Charlene.fic, Shumdw, Pndfam05, VoABot II, Mrld, Appraiser, H.sanat, EagleFan, Mkdw, DarK AQ, Rmislan, Bchertoff, Frank Kai Fat Chow, MartinBot, Jim.henderson, Aladdin Sane, Mike6271, Felipe1982, J.delanoy, TheWeasel, Public Menace, Mike.lifeguard, Zorry, STBotD, Cralar, VolkovBot, Davidwr, TXiKiBoT, JayC, Snowbot, Xx0033, ChrisWagoner, Monty845, SieBot, Bbouquet, Editus Reloaded, Toddst1, Pmboogie, Disklabs, Callidior, Shoombooly, Withouttrace, HighInBC, Mygerardromance, Wantnot, ClueBot, Orison316, The Thing That Should Not Be, Brandonjelinek, Altordwm, Dhendron, Ajcblyth, Natural Born Devastator, Karrde73, BlueAmethyst, Kushwadhwa, ResidueOfDesign, KesslerInternational, Jasperloco, Dekisugi, DanielPharos, Apparition11, XLinkBot, PeterFisk, Dianeburley, Srhinesmith, Cupids wings, Enarche, Addbot, L33tb0b, Jafeluv, MrOllie, LaaknorBot, Glane23, Leucius, DigitalMediaInvestigators, Tide rolls, Drpickem, Yobot, Themfromspace, Pinephilips, Evans1982, Vardanbalyan, AnomieBOT, Jim1138, Grolltech, Materialscientist, Santoshrautforensic, Vicpirate, Aneah, Roux-HG, Xqbot, Xeon06, GrouchoBot, Kesslerintl, Amaury, Locobot, Har-Magedon, .eXotech, Richard BB, Bmgoldbe, Janguilano, FrescoBot, Digitalx86, Nageh, HJ Mitchell, Aa999uk, Finalius, Jbeacontec, Glorymanu, Citation bot 1, Xxglennxx, Action grrl, Schoetti, CB79, Gdardick, Tbhotch, Semanresu, Woogee, RjwilmsiBot, Alexandru47, Rodolico, Jwbang, Rasriis~enwiki, TrudySinclaire, ISFCE, DASHBot, EmausBot, Daskalak, Immunize, Pacifistpanda, Rl244, TuHan-Bot, Dcirovic, Iamsquare, LinuxAngel, TOMA4ATO MONSTAH, Diana.todi, Suryatejag, Hazard-SJ, Bulldawg9908, Christina Silverman, Digicurator, Mynksh, Ericjhuber, ChuispastonBot, MacStep, ClueBot NG, Dfarrell07, Robklpd, Widr, Jonnychu, Helpful Pixie Bot, BG19bot, Pneidig, Jonathankrause, Wafoijoi99, CitationCleanerBot, Forensicsguru, Richu jose, ChrisGualtieri, Khazar2, SNAAAAKE!!, Cadava14, Phagen6368, Fuebar, Kwisha, Jamesx12345, Tdavidwood, Karl Obayi, I am One of Many, Enock4seth, Milicevic01, Int80, Consultantforensics, ForensicRA, Amritchhetrib, NottNott, YiFeiBot, Clevername462, Raviteja.addepalli, Duffit5, Monkbot, DataForensics, Professornova, KH-1, Alexandritechrysoberyl, KasparBot, CommentsEditor, Scifry1, Anticrypt, 20editor16, Shellbags56 and Anonymous: 434

- **Indicator of compromise** *Source:* https://en.wikipedia.org/wiki/Indicator_of_compromise?oldid=666037196 *Contributors:* Cloud200, Snori, BG19bot, Jantdm and Anonymous: 1

- **Anti-computer forensics** *Source:* https://en.wikipedia.org/wiki/Anti-computer_forensics?oldid=699399014 *Contributors:* SonofRage, PatrickFisher, Apokrif, GregorB, Panoptical, Wavelength, Family Guy Guy, DragonHawk, GraemeL, SmackBot, Elonka, Frap, Bwpach, Webucation, Iridescent, JForget, Gregbard, ErrantX, BetacommandBot, Fireice, Destynova, EMT1871, Deor, Triwbe, Shoombooly, XLinkBot, Thatguyflint, Crodenberg, MrOllie, Yobot, Materialscientist, NirajBhawnani, FrescoBot, IO Device, Feldermouse, RayBo95, Helpful Pixie Bot, Tastic007, PhnomPencil, Hlbgle, OctaviaYounger and Anonymous: 30

- **Anubisnetworks** *Source:* https://en.wikipedia.org/wiki/Anubisnetworks?oldid=649428940 *Contributors:* RJFJR, Malcolma, SmackBot, Stefan2, Rettetast, Nono64, Jojalozzo, WordyGirl90, Niceguyedc, Osarius, Yobot, FrescoBot, Mean as custard, Ruidiogoserra and Anonymous: 8

- **Autopsy (software)** *Source:* https://en.wikipedia.org/wiki/Autopsy_(software)?oldid=698416042 *Contributors:* Anthony Appleyard, JLaTondre, Pokey5945, MadmanBot, Wickorama, Palosirkka, Vacation9, Lugia2453, Pw5001 and Anonymous: 4

- **Certified Computer Examiner** *Source:* https://en.wikipedia.org/wiki/Certified_Computer_Examiner?oldid=590499795 *Contributors:* Pnm, Joncare, Rich Farmbrough, RJFJR, Pegship, Domthedude001, Emeraude, Addbot, Yobot, Autoerrant and Anonymous: 4

- **Computer and network surveillance** *Source:* https://en.wikipedia.org/wiki/Computer_and_network_surveillance?oldid=704112874 *Contributors:* Ubiquity, Modster, Pnm, Kku, Notheruser, Kingturtle, Smack, Novum, Ww, Fredrik, RedWolf, Gracefool, Wmahan, Andycjp, Beland, TonyW, Corti, Rich Farmbrough, ZeroOne, CanisRufus, Stesmo, ZayZayEM, Valar, Alansohn, Eleland, ReyBrujo, Versageek, Bobrayner, Mindmatrix, Rjwilmsi, Haya shiloh, Jrtayloriv, Intgr, Bgwhite, RussBot, Gardar Rurak, Bachrach44, Joel7687, Emijrp, Zzuuzz, Arthur Rubin, Rurik, Rwwww, SmackBot, Bluebot, GoldDragon, Adpete, Can't sleep, clown will eat me, Frap, Gamgee, Mion, Clicketyclack, Beetstra, Sander Säde, CmdrObot, JohnCD, Dreaded Walrus, Ingolfson, Techie guru, Magioladitis, Bongwarrior, Fedia, Elinruby, Atulsnischal, AVRS, CliffC, CommonsDelinker, Maurice Carbonaro, Hodja Nasreddin, Crakkpot, Demizh, Jeepday, AntiSpamBot, NewEnglandYankee, Andy Marchbanks, TreasuryTag, ServeNow, Pwnage8, PeetMoss, Qworty, MunkyJuce69, Svick, ClueBot, The Thing That Should Not Be, IoptaBan, WalterGR, Mlaffs, DumZiBoT, XLinkBot, Jasonma84, Melab-1, Ente75, MrOllie, Jarble, Legobot, Yobot, Vividupper66, AnomieBOT, LilHelpa, PansikMaZer, Ellipi, Alialiac, FrescoBot, 2dsea, M2545, PigFlu Oink, Lotje, RjwilmsiBot, Rollins83, John of Reading, Érico, H3llBot, W163, Ego White Tray, ClueBot NG, North Atlanticist Usonian, BG19bot, Sprinting faster, MusikAnimal, Meclee, BattyBot, ChrisGualtieri, Artem12345, TimMouraveiko, Jemappelleungarcon, I am One of Many, Ms. Anthropic, Majidmec, Someone not using his real name, Dannyruthe, Coreyemotela, Fixture, Itsalleasy, 7Sidz, The f18hornet, Monkbot, Ennykonto, Digitalzoo, Wallace McDonald, KH-1, Qin Xue, Starfire2999, Ghost Lourde, Johngreenaway, Hampton11235, Brendapallister, MagyVi, Nextstepsailing, CaseyMillerWiki, Cjllacuna, CAPTAIN RAJU, Nathan Bachman and Anonymous: 71

- **Computer Online Forensic Evidence Extractor** *Source:* https://en.wikipedia.org/wiki/Computer_Online_Forensic_Evidence_Extractor?oldid=693325378 *Contributors:* The Anome, Julesd, Thv, Holizz, Horkana, Douglasr007, Splat, Woohookitty, GregorB, Gaius Cornelius, Morphh, Welsh, EJSawyer, SmackBot, Sadads, Frap, Copysan, Davidhaha, Robofish, Peyre, Eastlaw, ErrantX, Thedarxide, Jdm64, Davidhorman,

Andreas Toth, Magioladitis, David Eppstein, 0utlaw, TheWeasel, Tokyogirl79, A.Arc, VolkovBot, Don4of4, Jamelan, Andy Dingley, Wikiborg2, Newt, Trivialist, Arjayay, SF007, Addbot, Dawynn, M.nelson, Download, Terrillja, Gilo1969, Breadtk, Down isthenew up, Tremaster, Decafme, ZéroBot, Wingman4l7, AndyTheGrump, JohnJamesWIlson, ClueBot NG, Mark Arsten, Craig131, Wywin, Tentinator, IrishSpook, Anzarshah, EditAvenger and Anonymous: 40

- **The Coroner's Toolkit** *Source:* https://en.wikipedia.org/wiki/The_Coroner'{}s_Toolkit?oldid=663593831 *Contributors:* Glenn, David Gerard, CanisRufus, Pol098, Hm2k, SmackBot, Thumperward, Frap, Skapur, ErrantX, NapoliRoma, Wax Tablet, Bongomatic, Boleyn, Addbot, Dawynn, Yobot, AnomieBOT, Xqbot, Kernel.package, Erik9, ChrisGualtieri and Anonymous: 4

- **Cyber Insider Threat** *Source:* https://en.wikipedia.org/wiki/Cyber_Insider_Threat?oldid=621625362 *Contributors:* TiMike, Discospinster, Nabla, Disavian, Magioladitis, Tassedethe, Yobot, AnomieBOT, VanishedUser sdu9aya9fasdsopa, SuperJew, Lotje, John of Reading, Khazar2 and Anonymous: 6

- **Cymmetria** *Source:* https://en.wikipedia.org/wiki/Cymmetria?oldid=703235484 *Contributors:* Fuzheado, Stesmo, Thedm, Wiae and BG19bot

- **Detekt** *Source:* https://en.wikipedia.org/wiki/Detekt?oldid=691353696 *Contributors:* Xaosflux, R'n'B, Hexafluoride, DoomCult and Anonymous: 2

- **Device configuration overlay** *Source:* https://en.wikipedia.org/wiki/Device_configuration_overlay?oldid=698185252 *Contributors:* Indefatigable, Ringbang, SmackBot, Frap, CmdrObot, Cydebot, BetacommandBot, Widefox, Leolaursen, Magioladitis, Kha0sangel, Dsimic, Przemek Klosowski, Matthiaspaul, Silicosaurus, Helpful Pixie Bot, Digitaloday, Monkbot and Anonymous: 5

- **DriveSavers** *Source:* https://en.wikipedia.org/wiki/DriveSavers?oldid=672741284 *Contributors:* Lquilter, Rpyle731, BusterD, Robofish, Johnchristopher, Elegie, AnomieBOT, CorporateM, Asukite, Binibro, Jaosnimpson, Jppcap, Unician, JenDCJen and Anonymous: 1

- **EnCase** *Source:* https://en.wikipedia.org/wiki/EnCase?oldid=702793429 *Contributors:* DNewhall, Necrothesp, BD2412, RussBot, Hm2k, Closedmouth, Rwwww, SmackBot, Narson, 豆豆豆, Michael miceli, A876, ErrantX, Richhoncho, Postlewaight, MelanieN, Magioladitis, VolkovBot, SieBot, Callidior, Csiemens, Star Mississippi, Addbot, MrZoolook, ConeyIslandWhite-fish, Tassedethe, Ettrig, Legobot, Legobot II, Wikiwikikid, WizardOfOz, Aneah, Fake4d, Contrapposto, TheTruth-2009, WibWobble, Action grrl, RjwilmsiBot, XaeroDegreaz, Eekerz, ZéroBot, Wingman4l7, Autoerrant, MainFrame, Helpful Pixie Bot, Justincheng12345-bot, CynSieWil and Anonymous: 35

- **FireEye** *Source:* https://en.wikipedia.org/wiki/FireEye?oldid=704693114 *Contributors:* Edward, Royce, Neutrality, Vsmith, Giraffedata, H2g2bob, Rjwilmsi, Mahlon, Bgwhite, ImGz, Arthur Rubin, John Broughton, SmackBot, FlashSheridan, Alepik, DouglasCalvert, Neelix, ErrantX, JustAGal, Struthious Bandersnatch, Pdbogen, DH85868993, Benhood, Aspects, Mojoworker, Stepheng3, Chzz, OlEnglish, Yobot, AnomieBOT, OlYeller21, Codwiki, Banej, Lotje, RjwilmsiBot, Fe4200, T3dkjn89q00vl02Cxp1kqs3x7, GoingBatty, Assembled, Wbm1058, BG19bot, Puramyun31, Socialmaven1, BattyBot, Frostmatthew, Iodide13, Kulandru mor, Infosec408, Wineshark, UKAmerican, Claudiaerecinos, OldCinjun, Lakun.patra, ForrestLyle, Tdk408, Sacred Falcon and Anonymous: 52

- **Forensic corporate collections** *Source:* https://en.wikipedia.org/wiki/Forensic_corporate_collections?oldid=624978895 *Contributors:* RussBot, Avalon, SmackBot, Addshore, Kvng, Alaibot, Fabrictramp, DGG, Rettetast, Katharineamy, Clashcityrocker21, Chris19910, Diannaa, Venustas 12, Papadonkey, Khazar2 and Anonymous: 2

- **Forensic search** *Source:* https://en.wikipedia.org/wiki/Forensic_search?oldid=700715802 *Contributors:* ViperSnake151, Chris the speller, Biscuittin, Apparition11, Yobot, FrescoBot, Dewritech, BG19bot, BattyBot, Mrt3366, George Adams Is Unique, Inom234, FoxyOrange, Awest262 and Anonymous: 1

- **Forensic Toolkit** *Source:* https://en.wikipedia.org/wiki/Forensic_Toolkit?oldid=699740682 *Contributors:* Canterbury Tail, Apoc2400, Rjwilmsi, ErrantX, Vmanoussos, Svick, Terrorist96, Dawynn, I dream of horses, DBigXray, HkLAtx and Anonymous: 13

- **HashKeeper** *Source:* https://en.wikipedia.org/wiki/HashKeeper?oldid=655160576 *Contributors:* Paul A, Gary, Kbolino, Intgr, Closedmouth, SmackBot, Betacommand, Bluebot, Frap, Cydebot, ErrantX, MarshBot, RainbowCrane, Salad Days, Pndfam05, Fabrictramp, Cander0000, Xhantar, Slash Firestorm, Cybercop22, Addbot, Lightbot, AnomieBOT, Jonmccune, NoNewsToday, Hedles, Casascius and Anonymous: 10

- **Host protected area** *Source:* https://en.wikipedia.org/wiki/Host_protected_area?oldid=704125972 *Contributors:* Dcljr, Indefatigable, Dimmer, Alexkon, Kim Meyrick, Kenyon, A D Monroe III, Firsfron, FlaBot, Petiatil, DragonHawk, Sandstein, SmackBot, Reedy, Colonies Chris, Frap, WRAR, Etienne lorrain, Cydebot, Ntsimp, A876, Stromdal, Lanchon, Varnent, DumZiBoT, Dsimic, Addbot, Rjaf29, CCFS, Mrpetewiki, Dzikasosna, Van Rijn, Dinamik-bot, Tremaster, Matthiaspaul, Helpful Pixie Bot, BG19bot, BattyBot and Anonymous: 32

- **Lastline** *Source:* https://en.wikipedia.org/wiki/Lastline?oldid=675570337 *Contributors:* Yobot, FrescoBot, BG19bot, Matthewjamesbaker and Bobhambrick

- **MAC times** *Source:* https://en.wikipedia.org/wiki/MAC_times?oldid=651280114 *Contributors:* Tero~enwiki, AlistairMcMillan, Bender235, PhilHibbs, Sietse Snel, Tmh, Guy Harris, Distantbody, Jonathan de Boyne Pollard, Kbdank71, Intgr, Alvin-cs, SmackBot, Rvcx, ErrantX, ACSE, Jadtnr1, Addbot, MrOllie, Yobot, AnomieBOT, Mschamschula, Wietse venema, ZéroBot, Prüm, BG19bot, Eidab, Mfpp, BattyBot, Techie007, Professornova and Anonymous: 15

- **MailXaminer** *Source:* https://en.wikipedia.org/wiki/MailXaminer?oldid=677232254 *Contributors:* Eclipsed, Natg 19, MatthewVanitas, AnomieBOT, Klbrain, BG19bot, DPL bot, Vincent60030, PotatoNinja and Jude Alouysis

- **Memory forensics** *Source:* https://en.wikipedia.org/wiki/Memory_forensics?oldid=616995500 *Contributors:* JustAGal, Fadesga, Mild Bill Hiccup, Dawynn, BG19bot, Sosthenes12, Int80, Lesser Cartographies and Anonymous: 3

- **Nuix** *Source:* https://en.wikipedia.org/wiki/Nuix?oldid=680041549 *Contributors:* C.Fred, Tmyroadctfig, Vealmince, Magioladitis, Addbot, FrescoBot, Jesse V., Khazar2, Miss Thingy and Anonymous: 5

- **Open Computer Forensics Architecture** *Source:* https://en.wikipedia.org/wiki/Open_Computer_Forensics_Architecture?oldid=649397114 *Contributors:* Bearcat, Thorwald, Fnorp, Tony1, Dicklyon, ErrantX, Faizhaider, Atownballer, Niceguyedc, Bunnyhop11, Aoidh, Robklpd, Pibara and BattyBot

- **PTK Forensics** *Source:* https://en.wikipedia.org/wiki/PTK_Forensics?oldid=695586792 *Contributors:* Raistolo, ErrantX, Nuwewsco, Magioladitis, Remco47, JL-Bot, FrescoBot, WKPdwatkins and Anonymous: 3

- **Registry Recon** *Source:* https://en.wikipedia.org/wiki/Registry_Recon?oldid=640683100 *Contributors:* MkhitarSparapet, Bgs876, Addbot and LittleWink

- **Digital Forensics Framework** *Source:* https://en.wikipedia.org/wiki/Digital_Forensics_Framework?oldid=695658201 *Contributors:* Alexf, Rjwilmsi, Derek R Bullamore, Lfstevens, Jerryobject, Flyer22 Reborn, Ironholds, Yobot, Alvin Seville, LittleWink, Animalparty, ClueBot NG, BG19bot, BattyBot, WikiRobert3, Udgover, SpiritualStar, Will722, Ellasaunders99, Fryman.jayce, Rynnovations, Evangelist Moses J Roderique, MontgomeryDiana, Pat kenny's slave trade, Alicja11willow, Sevnth, Alfaiha, Anushkanu, Fredharry1712, Einpedia, Sbjit.wiki and Anonymous: 3

- **SANS Investigative Forensics Toolkit** *Source:* https://en.wikipedia.org/wiki/SANS_Investigative_Forensics_Toolkit?oldid=634765575 *Contributors:* Zundark, Kubieziel, Tony1, Karrde73, Yobot, Xqbot, Ravendrop, I dream of horses, Dohn joe, ClueBot NG, BattyBot and Anonymous: 4

- **SecurityMetrics** *Source:* https://en.wikipedia.org/wiki/SecurityMetrics?oldid=687652778 *Contributors:* Faustus37, Teb728, SmackBot, A. B., CmdrObot, Cydebot, Johnpacklambert, Funandtrvl, WOSlinker, ImageRemovalBot, Grayfell, Download, Ben Ben, Yobot, AnomieBOT, Hairhorn, FrescoBot, Access Denied, SecurityMetrics, Msbaxter22, BG19bot, Cabljr, BattyBot, ChrisGualtieri, HarmonMama, Appelbaum~enwiki, Savvysecurity, Jasonhicks, Poppop1988 and Anonymous: 7

- **Selective file dumper** *Source:* https://en.wikipedia.org/wiki/Selective_file_dumper?oldid=638339542 *Contributors:* Glenn, Raistolo, NeilN, SmackBot, Frap, Schmloof, R'n'B, KingFanel, Addbot, Nannibas, Autoerrant, Lemnaminor and Anonymous: 7

- **The Sleuth Kit** *Source:* https://en.wikipedia.org/wiki/The_Sleuth_Kit?oldid=682072001 *Contributors:* Glenn, Ahunt, Hm2k, Mkurth, Raistolo, Cyrus Grisham, Rurik, SmackBot, Reedy, Bluebot, Frap, A876, ErrantX, Nick Number, Digevidence, Addbot, Dawynn, Wikiwikikid, Fake4d, Ts jem, Aoidh, Suffusion of Yellow, John of Reading, WKPdwatkins, Sfrands, ZéroBot, BG19bot, BattyBot, Pw5001 and Anonymous: 19

- **StegAlyzerAS** *Source:* https://en.wikipedia.org/wiki/StegAlyzerAS?oldid=588533819 *Contributors:* Bearcat, Malcolma, Tookiewana, KylieTastic and Jsfouche

- **Trend Micro** *Source:* https://en.wikipedia.org/wiki/Trend_Micro?oldid=699849528 *Contributors:* Plop, Chrisjj, RedWolf, Delpino, Pabouk, Fudoreaper, Zigger, Greyweather, TonyW, CGorman~enwiki, Zhangleisme, Brianhe, Rich Farmbrough, YUL89YYZ, Susvolans, Richi, Water Bottle, Hoary, Woohookitty, Thorpe, Pol098, Mb1000, Rjwilmsi, The Rambling Man, YurikBot, Moocat, Romanc19s, Gareth Jones, Voidxor, Black Falcon, Ernestnywang, SmackBot, JohnRussell, J o, Alepik, Xaosflux, Gilliam, Slo-mo, Snori, Htchien, Tohma, Frap, OrphanBot, Alriode, BoKu, MartinRe, Diasimon2003, TPO-bot, Ricky@36, Will Beback, Guyjohnston, Catapult, IronGargoyle, Inoesomestuff, Peyre, Iridescent, Winkydink, Joergvader, Herenthere, Raamin, Bubba 83835, Danhm, Second Quantization, Mentifisto, WinBot, Quintote, THEunique, Mpr1234, Scchiang, Rentir, Saganaki-, Lifanxi~enwiki, CliffC, Mark Rosenthal, Bongomatic, AstroHurricane001, Maurice Carbonaro, Wikicharliehorse, Spacecookies, Althepal, DMCer, ACSE, M ran66, Kww, Runrun 923, Ronpangan, Metadigm, Kmverdi, SieBot, VVVBot, Eastersomething, Ham Pastrami, Jerryobject, WiebeVanDerWorp~enwiki, Gnfgb2, Aspects, Kanonkas, L337h1um, Martarius, Kliu1, Niceguyedc, Ottawahitech, Rockfang, Stepshep, -Midorihana-, John Nevard, Tolheiser, Ark25, Stepheng3, SF007, XLinkBot, SandiMeyer2008, Svgalbertian, Addbot, Kankachi1980Kan, BenTrotsky, JEN9841, JamieRoe, Yobot, Legobot II, QueenCake, Wonderfl, Esoteric Rogue, AnomieBOT, Ciphers, 9258fahsflkh917fas, Ulric1313, Clarafaie, Xqbot, Erik9, Vlambie, FrescoBot, D'ohBot, HamburgerRadio, Singaporesuperboy, Tornedo500, Winterst, Apple1loop, Jandalhandler, J123456ddd, SchreyP, Lotje, Sahil16, 777sms, Forces91, UseYourGreymatter, Kkm010, ClueBot NG, BG19bot, Compfreak7, Aloysius Sebastian, MeanMotherJr, Dark Silver Crow, Cryptodd, Epicgenius, Zombie88, Nozic74, Lythronaxargestes, IdlePlayground, ArturZ72, Ishan Mathur 18, RGuy02, RobbyCase, AMSN, Case2394, Wikipedia wangwang and Anonymous: 142

- **VMRay** *Source:* https://en.wikipedia.org/wiki/VMRay?oldid=695696903 *Contributors:* Bearcat, AllyD, BoKu, Magioladitis, Cloeven and BG19bot

- **Volatility (memory forensics)** *Source:* https://en.wikipedia.org/wiki/Volatility_(memory_forensics)?oldid=640958306 *Contributors:* Bearcat, Malcolma, Rwalker, Martarius, EagerToddler39, Sosthenes12, Int80, Buergich and Anonymous: 1

- **WindowsSCOPE** *Source:* https://en.wikipedia.org/wiki/WindowsSCOPE?oldid=637969118 *Contributors:* Yobot, Jeffage0 and Anonymous: 2

39.5.2 Images

- **File:2010-05-14-USCYBERCOM_Logo.jpg** *Source:* https://upload.wikimedia.org/wikipedia/commons/3/3a/2010-05-14-USCYBERCOM_Logo.jpg *License:* Public domain *Contributors:* Department of Defense *Original artist:* http://www.defense.gov/home/features/2010/0410_cybersec/images/cybercom_seal_large1.jpg Department of Defense

- **File:Ambox_important.svg** *Source:* https://upload.wikimedia.org/wikipedia/commons/b/b4/Ambox_important.svg *License:* Public domain *Contributors:* Own work, based off of Image:Ambox scales.svg *Original artist:* Dsmurat (talk · contribs)

- **File:AnubisNetworks_new_logo.jpg** *Source:* https://upload.wikimedia.org/wikipedia/en/0/0e/AnubisNetworks_new_logo.jpg *License:* Fair use *Contributors:* https://www.anubisnetworks.com *Original artist:* ?

- **File:Arsenal_Recon_Logo.png** *Source:* https://upload.wikimedia.org/wikipedia/en/a/a9/Arsenal_Recon_Logo.png *License:* Fair use *Contributors:* Arsenal Recon *Original artist:* ?

- **File:AusFactory.svg** *Source:* https://upload.wikimedia.org/wikipedia/commons/b/b4/AusFactory.svg *License:* Public domain *Contributors:* Made from public domain images File:Factory.svg and File:Flag of Australia.svg *Original artist:* User:Slashme

- **File:Boundless_Informant_data_collection.svg** *Source:* https://upload.wikimedia.org/wikipedia/commons/5/5b/Boundless_Informant_data_collection.svg *License:* CC0 *Contributors:* BlankMap-World6.svg *Original artist:* Rezonansowy

- **File:CIA.svg** *Source:* https://upload.wikimedia.org/wikipedia/commons/2/23/CIA.svg *License:* Public domain *Contributors:* http://www.law.cornell.edu/uscode/50/403m.html *Original artist:* United States federal government

- **File:Commons-logo.svg** *Source:* https://upload.wikimedia.org/wikipedia/en/4/4a/Commons-logo.svg *License:* CC-BY-SA-3.0 *Contributors:* ? *Original artist:* ?

- **File:Crystal_Clear_app_browser.png** *Source:* https://upload.wikimedia.org/wikipedia/commons/f/fe/Crystal_Clear_app_browser.png *License:* LGPL *Contributors:* All Crystal icons were posted by the author as LGPL on kde-look *Original artist:* Everaldo Coelho and YellowIcon

- **File:Crystal_Clear_app_database.png** *Source:* https://upload.wikimedia.org/wikipedia/commons/4/40/Crystal_Clear_app_database.png *License:* LGPL *Contributors:* All Crystal Clear icons were posted by the author as LGPL on kde-look; *Original artist:* Everaldo Coelho and YellowIcon;

- **File:Crystal_kpackage.png** *Source:* https://upload.wikimedia.org/wikipedia/commons/4/40/Crystal_kpackage.png *License:* LGPL *Contributors:* All Crystal icons were posted by the author as LGPL on kde-look *Original artist:* Everaldo Coelho (YellowIcon);

- **File:Cymmetria_Logo_150x150.png** *Source:* https://upload.wikimedia.org/wikipedia/commons/1/1d/Cymmetria_Logo_150x150.png *License:* CC BY-SA 3.0 *Contributors:* Cymmetria Website *Original artist:* Cymmetria

- **File:Dave_DeWalt,_CEO_and_Chairman_of_the_Board_from_acrofan.jpg** *Source:* https://upload.wikimedia.org/wikipedia/commons/5/5a/Dave_DeWalt%2C_CEO_and_Chairman_of_the_Board_from_acrofan.jpg *License:* CC BY-SA 3.0 *Contributors:* http://www.acrofan.com/ko-kr/commerce/content/main.ksp?mode=view&cate=0103&wd=20130618&ucode=0001030202&page=1&keyfield=&keyword= *Original artist:* acrofan.com

- **File:Detekt_Logo.png** *Source:* https://upload.wikimedia.org/wikipedia/commons/9/95/Detekt_Logo.png *License:* GPL *Contributors:* https://github.com/botherder/detekt/blob/master/gui/static/logo.png *Original artist:* Claudio Guarnieri

- **File:Edit-clear.svg** *Source:* https://upload.wikimedia.org/wikipedia/en/f/f2/Edit-clear.svg *License:* Public domain *Contributors:* The *Tango! Desktop Project.* *Original artist:*
The people from the Tango! project. And according to the meta-data in the file, specifically: "Andreas Nilsson, and Jakub Steiner (although minimally)."

- **File:EnCase_logo.jpg** *Source:* https://upload.wikimedia.org/wikipedia/en/d/d5/EnCase_logo.jpg *License:* Fair use *Contributors:*
From the copyright holder, Guidance Software.
Original artist: ?

- **File:Encase.png** *Source:* https://upload.wikimedia.org/wikipedia/en/2/2a/Encase.png *License:* Fair use *Contributors:*
User created screenshot
Original artist: ?

- **File:FTK_logo.jpg** *Source:* https://upload.wikimedia.org/wikipedia/en/5/52/FTK_logo.jpg *License:* Fair use *Contributors:*
The logo is from the www.accessdata.com website. Access Data *Original artist:* ?

- **File:Factory_1b.svg** *Source:* https://upload.wikimedia.org/wikipedia/commons/b/b6/Factory_1b.svg *License:* CC-BY-SA-3.0 *Contributors:* PNG version on the English Wikipedia *Original artist:* Dtbohrer, updated to SVG by Tomtheman5

- **File:Fbi_duquesne.jpg** *Source:* https://upload.wikimedia.org/wikipedia/commons/0/07/Fbi_duquesne.jpg *License:* Public domain *Contributors:* ? *Original artist:* ?

- **File:FireEye,_Inc._logo.svg** *Source:* https://upload.wikimedia.org/wikipedia/en/1/1e/FireEye%2C_Inc._logo.svg *License:* Fair use *Contributors:* http://www.fireeye.com/resources/pdfs/fireeye-advanced-threat-protection.pdf *Original artist:* ?

- **File:Flag_of_Australia.svg** *Source:* https://upload.wikimedia.org/wikipedia/en/b/b9/Flag_of_Australia.svg *License:* Public domain *Contributors:* ? *Original artist:* ?

- **File:Flag_of_Canada.svg** *Source:* https://upload.wikimedia.org/wikipedia/en/c/cf/Flag_of_Canada.svg *License:* PD *Contributors:* ? *Original artist:* ?

- **File:Flag_of_France.svg** *Source:* https://upload.wikimedia.org/wikipedia/en/c/c3/Flag_of_France.svg *License:* PD *Contributors:* ? *Original artist:* ?

- **File:Flag_of_Germany.svg** *Source:* https://upload.wikimedia.org/wikipedia/en/b/ba/Flag_of_Germany.svg *License:* PD *Contributors:* ? *Original artist:* ?

- **File:Flag_of_Japan.svg** *Source:* https://upload.wikimedia.org/wikipedia/en/9/9e/Flag_of_Japan.svg *License:* PD *Contributors:* ? *Original artist:* ?

- **File:Flag_of_New_Zealand.svg** *Source:* https://upload.wikimedia.org/wikipedia/commons/3/3e/Flag_of_New_Zealand.svg *License:* Public domain *Contributors:* http://www.mch.govt.nz/files/NZ%20Flag%20-%20proportions.JPG *Original artist:* Zscout370, Hugh Jass and many others

- **File:Flag_of_the_United_Kingdom.svg** *Source:* https://upload.wikimedia.org/wikipedia/en/a/ae/Flag_of_the_United_Kingdom.svg *License:* PD *Contributors:* ? *Original artist:* ?

- **File:Folder_Hexagonal_Icon.svg** *Source:* https://upload.wikimedia.org/wikipedia/en/4/48/Folder_Hexagonal_Icon.svg *License:* Cc-by-sa-3.0 *Contributors:* ? *Original artist:* ?

- **File:Free_Software_Portal_Logo.svg** *Source:* https://upload.wikimedia.org/wikipedia/commons/6/67/Nuvola_apps_emacs_vector.svg *License:* LGPL *Contributors:*

- Nuvola_apps_emacs.png *Original artist:* Nuvola_apps_emacs.png: David Vignoni

- **File:Gnome-searchtool.svg** *Source:* https://upload.wikimedia.org/wikipedia/commons/1/1e/Gnome-searchtool.svg *License:* LGPL *Contributors:* http://ftp.gnome.org/pub/GNOME/sources/gnome-themes-extras/0.9/gnome-themes-extras-0.9.0.tar.gz *Original artist:* David Vignoni

39.5.3   Content license